DEFENDING *the* PURITY *of* WORSHIP

PHIL KING

Defending the
Purity of Worship

by Phil King

ISBN-13: 978-0692629604 (Phil King)
ISBN-10: 0692629602

Book Website
www.philkingmusic.com
Email: phil@philkingmusic.com

Send feedback on the book to:
phil@philkingmusic.com

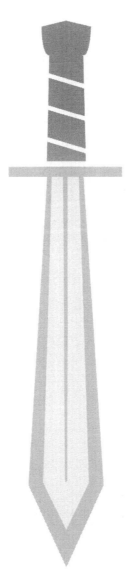

DEFENDING *the* PURITY *of* WORSHIP

PHIL KING

Defending the Purity of Worship

by Phil King

About This Book

You can't have a healthy church without healthy worship. If you are a worshipper of Jesus Christ, a worker in the Christian music industry, a part of a worship team, or a pastor, this book is for you.

It is an alarming fact that we are in a time when the American Church is being more entertained than ever. Why is this alarming? Because, while the Church is being so entertained on Sunday mornings, the art of entertaining the Presence of the Lord has nearly been lost. *Defending the Purity of Worship* is a tool that will help any worship team get back to the core of worship so that they may bring the best and purest adoration to the Lord. What's within this book is so critical and timely for the American Church.

Until we are all made aware of the things that may be holding us back from worshipping in Spirit and in Truth, we will never get there. Within this book are powerful teachings, filled with amazing truths on worship from the Word of God, that will help you get there. There is also practical insight from Phil that will equip you to be highly effective and efficient whether you are a member or leader of a worship team.

About The Author

Phil King is an emerging voice in the American Church. He grew up in California and began leading worship at the age of 15.

He is a singer-songwriter who's passion is to create and present the best worship to Jesus.

Phil has ministered extensively across the United States and abroad for several years as he aims to bring a message of purity and holiness to his generation.

With a heart to raise up leaders, Phil also actively trains and equips worshippers and worship leaders who will minister before the Lord.

Phil has worked alongside many influential musicians including Michael W. Smith, Leeland, Lindell Cooley (Brownsville Revival) and others.

His music is available on most major platforms (iTunes, Google Play, Spotify, etc). Learn more at philkingmusic.com.

Table of Contents

Acknowledgements

Before we dive into *Defending the Purity of Worship* it is important that I honor those God has used to shape me into the man I am today. I am so thankful for every friend; every mentor and every Pastor He has placed in my life to watch over what I do.

But far before any of these men in my life it is God's Holy Spirit and the precious blood of Jesus that has made me into the man I am today. I make it my goal to not cling to anyone or anything more tightly than I cling to Jesus Christ and His cross. Without His love there most certainly would have been no hope for me to change. Thanks to God's mercy and forgiveness, the way has been revealed for us to become more and more like Him.

We ought to be so thankful for every moment on Earth that our Father gives us and live wisely using everything we have to shine for Jesus. *"For in him we live and move and have our being."* (Acts 17:28 NIV) And how do we show Him we truly are thankful for all He has done? By living for Him. *"As I learn your righteous regulations, I will thank you (God) by living as I should."*

(Psalms 119:7 NLT) I thank the Lord often that I do not have to run this race alone. In this day and age when the earth is so filled with darkness what a joy it is to know that I am not alone in standing for Jesus Christ. *"Since God so loved us, we also ought to love one another."* (1 John 4:11 NIV)

I always have thought to myself that the greatest leaders in the Church are always the ones that are simply the best followers of Christ. Men who follow after Him with excellence are the kind of men that I want to follow myself and learn from. I realize that without godly relationships like this in my life I would not be where I am at today. Much of the content of this book came directly from me spending time with the Holy Spirit, but many other parts were caught by simply being around these great men that I am about to give honor to. **The mark of a great spiritual leader is that they live a life that inspires you to draw nearer to Jesus.** Being around a true leader in the Kingdom just makes you want more of God.

I would like to begin by honoring the man in my life who I looked up to growing up and still do today. He is my beloved grandfather, Pastor Charles Combs. You were always the one person I wanted to be around as a little boy. I saw the hand of God on your life from as early on as I can remember and I have always admired your strength and your character. I am thankful for all of the sacrifices you have made for our family. You are a model of integrity. Through the years I've always been able to look to you for support and count on you. Surely you are standing on the Solid Rock. Everyone who knows you can see you have clean hands and a pure heart. Going to visit you and grandma as a young boy, when you all pastored at The Brooklyn Tabernacle, changed my life. It was under your watch in California that I had my first encounters with the Holy Spirit. I came to have an awareness of my life's calling to love Jesus with all my heart. Thank you so much for all you have done for our family and for the Lord. I love you Papa.

Pastor Lindell Cooley, just to be in the same room as you is such a blessing. I am so thankful for how real you are and how you preach God's word with such boldness. You will always be a trusted voice to my generation. Thank you for showing me everything you have shown me about worship and about touching God's heart. You should be getting some sort of credit for this book. There were many things I always felt in my spirit that I could not put into words until I met you. Besides all of the deep stuff, I am so thankful to know such a great man of God that makes me laugh so much and tells me how I should **really** be singing the songs I write, haha! I love you Pastor Lindell.

Mike Spears, what a blessing you and your precious family

are to my life. Ilse, London and Dakota, you all make me so happy and I enjoy every moment I get to be around you all. Mike, I can't say that I know too many people who are more inspirational to be around than you. What an amazing gift of vision God has put on your life. Thank you so much for your incredible input towards this project. You have truly blessed my ministry. I cannot say thank you enough for the answer you have been to so many of my prayers. Thank you so much!

Finally, I would like to thank all of the local churches across America and abroad who have invited me to come and minister. Each and every one of you is such a special and significant part of the Body of Christ, and I do not take it lightly that you all continue to open up your platforms to me. I take ministering to you all very seriously, and I will continue to live a life that follows hard after Christ with clean hands and a pure heart. May this book not only be a blessing to you but to your entire church family.

Introduction

Thank you so much for taking the time to read this book. God has burdened my life to be a living example of what purely loving God looks like. A great part of this is defending the purity of worship. To defend worship's purity should be a desire of every Christian's heart. God asked me one night when I was driving down a highway in Tennessee "Son, what do you want the future of worship to look like in America?" I thought long and hard before giving Him an answer. I thought about all the new and different sounds we could make, all the ways we could reform and what we as worship leaders could do to direct the attention of the Bride back to Jesus.

But then it hit me – suddenly I knew without a shadow of a doubt what I wanted the future of worship in America to look like. I cried out my answer to God's question in my car, "Father! Our hearts! It does not matter to me what we look like or what we sound like, just as long as our hearts, the heart of Your Church, is purely and madly in love with You." If that was what the future of our worship looked like I would be satisfied and I know that everything else would take care of itself. When our hearts are right before the King, the songs of worship come out naturally all on their own.

PHIL KING

Much of the American Church today has become imbalanced and has fallen in love with the things of the world. She is trying to worship her God in similar ways to how the world worships her false idols. Unfortunately, in much of the American Church, there is the same kind of emphasis placed on being a celebrity, like in the world. How is this so when Christ showed us being a servant is the highest honor of all? Being a servant no longer carries any honor in the American Church. Many of the mindsets that have snuck their way into the American Church are not from Christ but from Satan.

You know, the Church shouldn't really resemble the world at all and that's a whole separate book altogether. We have to be very careful where our affections lie because the reality is that every single person right now on planet Earth is worshipping. In fact, it is impossible for anyone to not be worshipping. Everyone's mind is meditating, everyone's heart is longing and every person's soul is exalting. Every last bit of this inward activity is centered on something. It may be vain and evil. It may be pure and true. Nonetheless, no one, not even a single person, has the power to not worship.

To know exactly what it is that someone is worshipping, just find out what it is they put the most value on. The thing in anyone's life that holds the most value is the object of his or her worship. Now it makes much more sense as to why

Jesus would say that we must love Him even more than our own families. What is it that moves your heart most? What is it that you treasure most? That, my friends is the object of your worship.

There are many things today that are mistakenly labeled as healthy worship in the Church that really are not healthy at all. Things that have not even a hint of Christ-likeness. Every instance where the focus of worship is something other than Jesus is an instance where the worship of an idol is what's really going on. Worship teams and worship leaders: We were not created to lift up our own names or to adore our own image. Worship is all about our hearts being focused on Jesus and magnifying Him alone.

There is a common belief in the Church today that worship is all about the music. As this book will unveil, this is simply not the Truth. Worship starts with what we are doing inwardly and music is just an outward medium that serves as an outlet for the much deeper adoration in our hearts. Worship has never been about a sound as much as it has been about the heart. Without the heart in the right place the sound is meaningless.

Worship teams and worship leaders: I wrote this book because I love you all so much. Every word is for your growth and everything that may seem challenging is actually for your benefit. There will be things in this book that will be hard to swallow…things that will put you to the test. I promise you that every area where this book challenges you is an area that God wants to put His finger on, in order to bring healing to your life and to your ministry. God desires to expose any darkness that can easily ensnare us, not to shame us, but to bring wholeness.

There are many wounded worship teams across America today that my heart is broken for. Many are the horrible attacks that the enemy has unleashed against them because he wants them to become discouraged and silent. I hope that each and every chapter in this book will bring great healing and breakthrough to you and your worship team. Would you pray this simple prayer before we get started?

"Father, here I am.
Soften my heart to hear and receive all you
have for me as I read this book.
In the name of Jesus, amen."

1

Obedience, Not Talent, Shows God That We Love Him

In Matthew 25 Jesus tells a story of three men being given talents from a wealthy master. Two of the three men who were given talents were obedient with them, while one was not. The Bible calls the two faithful servants "wise." For these two wise servants it was not merely having the talent that impressed God but their obedience.

The first thing we need to know about defending the purity of worship is that our own gifts and talents can never impress the One who made them. That's impossible. A heart that truly loves God will always express itself through something that far surpasses talent; and that something is called obedience.

God gives talent to reveal what is actually hidden deep inside someone's heart. Yes, what someone does with their talent reveals who they really are on the inside and who they love to serve on the outside. So if God has not brought increase to your talent maybe it's for a reason. He could be protecting the fate of your soul.

Whether you agree with it or not, there is not a single thing in this universe that can escape bringing God glory. Consider even the most awful and perverse creature of all, Satan. His most despicable hour of rebellion will simply be used as a tool to bring God even more glory. How can this be? His most destructive rampage at the end of time will be the very curtain call for the Church to ready herself for the return of her King. His most despicable rebellion will be the very darkness and backdrop upon which the Glory of the Lord will arise. Glory does not arise and shine on nothingness - it shines and breaks upon darkness. Nothing is wasted, not even a single moment. Everything and everyone is used for the magnification and the glory of the Lord, whether they like it or not.

So, here is my big question to every passionate worshipper reading this book: If He can take even the darkness and cause it to bring Him glory, what then separates us who are called His children from those who dwell in darkness? The answer is 'obedience' - our utter refusal to compromise with sin. As God's children, we are called to obey our Heavenly Father, above all things.

According to Jesus, obedience is how we really tell Him

that we love Him. He said it Himself - *"If you love me, keep my commands."* (John 14:15 NLT) Truly, the best way we can display our love for Him as worshippers is to obey Him.

A worship leader who is okay with living in disobedience, while still offering sacrifices of worship to God, is not pleasing to the Lord. To do this kind of thing is to align yourself with the heart of Saul. God said to Saul through His prophet Samuel: *"Does the LORD delight in burnt offerings and sacrifices as much as in obeying the LORD? To obey is better than sacrifice, and to heed is better than the fat of rams."* (2 Samuel 15:22 NIV) Being okay with sin and thinking you can still touch God's heart by offering worship to Him is a big mistake and often a deadly trap. God can never be deceived in this way.

Always make sure that your talents do not take precedence over your obedience unto the Word of God or else your talents will be rendered worthless. The wicked servant in Matthew 25 who showed no diligence and no obedience took his talent and buried it in the ground. **Have you ever stopped to wonder why he buried it in the ground?** Why the ground? Why didn't he put it under his bed? Why didn't he put it in a safe? Or why didn't he hide it in something other than dirt? I believe if Jesus had told this same parable today he would have said something like this: "The wicked servant took his talent and hid it in the ground - exactly six feet under…" The reason why Jesus said the wicked servant buried his talent in the ground is because he took it to the grave with him. **If you want to find all the unused talents that Jesus gave to many, but they hid them in fear, just go visit a graveyard anywhere in the world and you can find them all buried there.** Jesus then said that the master returned after a **long time** to see how the three servants used his money. Jesus is the Master and this represents His return to the Earth. The servants standing before the Lord in the parable represents Christ judging our works on Earth.

In today's world a wicked servant is the kind of man who lives his life attending church and does nothing more. He is perfectly content taking up space on a Sunday morning pew, while never applying the Word of God or the power of God to his life. The wicked servant is the kind of man who never takes his God-given talent and seeks out what he can do with it to spread the Good News of the Kingdom. **Many of us who are alive today will pass away before Jesus returns. Our bodies will lie buried in the grave until the trumpet sounds, but our talents do not have to lie there buried with us.** Do not be like the wicked servant and take your talent to the grave with you. Apply obedience to your life and the Holy Spirit will show you step by step how to become a good and faithful servant.

FOOD FOR THOUGHT

QUESTION & ANSWER TIME

1. Where does your obedience to God rank in your life?

2. Do you lead worship or serve at a church on Sundays and then willingly disobey God during the week?

3. What can you do with the talents God has given you to be obedient unto the call on your life to serve in God's Kingdom?

2

Blind Spots of the Anointing

Whenever a person is driving a motor vehicle there are certain viewpoints that are hidden from their sight because of how the car is built. These hard to see angles that are usually behind the driver to the left and to the right are known as "blind spots."

After seeing many things in my young life, I can assure you that anyone will have an easier time with the blind spots of an 18-wheeler semi truck than the blind-spots that come with the anointing.

Anointed worshippers, if you want to keep your life pure and finish your race strong you need to be made as aware as possible of the dangers that come when you are a carrier of the anointing.

We all know that those who do not learn from history are doomed to repeat it. So in this chapter I would like to talk a little bit about the histories of three highly anointed men of God: Jehu, King Saul and Samson. If we take the time to study what is written down in the Word of God about these men we will save ourselves from a great deal of trouble.

Jehu, King Saul and Samson were all highly anointed men of God. They each did mighty things for God and were used to bring great breakthrough for the nation of Israel. If any of these three men were in a fight against an enemy it was highly likely that they were going to come out on top because God was with them. One of these men was even the first King of Israel. But in the end all three of these highly anointed men became total failures.

How did these three highly anointed men end up as total failures? They bought into the lie that because they were anointed they could afford to get by with some compromise. Worshippers and worship leaders cannot afford to fall into this same trap. **Having an anointing on your life does not make you exempt from obeying all the laws of the Kingdom.** In the same regard, being anointed to lead does not make you exempt from being a servant.

Jehu, King Saul and Samson believed that because God was with them they had an excuse for sin. Many worship leaders, even well known Church figures, have succumbed to this very same trap. The anointing is one of the most precious gifts someone can receive from Heaven. It is never to be seen as a token that puts someone above the Word of God. If we view the anointing as something that puts us above God's word, we will lead ourselves straight into failure. We must always remember that we are anointed to serve the Lord and not ourselves.

In summary, if you are someone that carries the anointing of God you need to be extra careful. *"From everyone who has been given much, much will be demanded; and from the one who has been entrusted with much, much more will be asked."* This is what Jesus said in Luke 12:48 NLT. The anointing of God is never given to anyone by accident. It is entrusted to people for the powerful purpose of carrying out Heaven's agenda on Earth and the only way we can be sure to do this is by being obedient. We must never lose sight of obedience as we carry the anointing of God on our lives.

FOOD FOR THOUGHT
QUESTION & ANSWER TIME

....

1. What blind spots do you have in your life that if left unchecked could bring about your destruction?

2. Do you have accountability in your life to whom you can answer to for your own protection and longevity?

3

ᥱᨏᥱ

It Was Crowd Pleasing
That Killed Jesus

"*So Pilate, wishing to satisfy the crowd, released for them Barabbas, and having scourged Jesus, he delivered him to be crucified.*" (Mark 15:15 ESV) There is a key phrase in this verse that led to Jesus being crucified: "*So Pilate, wishing to satisfy the crowd...*"

When your heart's desire is to satisfy the crowd you will inevitably put Jesus on the cross and scourge Him. There are only two things that you can serve in life, the world or God. Christians who think that there may be a possibility of peace between the world and Heaven should know that the dark unseen powers of this world, in all of their pride, only want Jesus in one condition: Crucified. Truly pleasing God requires a humble heart and an unwillingness to please the prideful spirit of the world.

Worshippers - whatever it is that you desire to satisfy the most is what you are really worshipping. So what are you living to satisfy the most? Is it the crowd or God? If you are a worshipper, then your aim should be to please only one. Do not worry about, or get caught up in, what the world says about you. It does not matter. Do not worry about what those with cold religious hearts are saying about you either. If people treated Jesus that way back then, should you expect to be treated any differently now?

Are you pleasing God and obeying Him? Are you worshipping with the sole aim of touching His heart? If your answer is yes to both of these questions, then you are completely satisfactory to God, and what else matters more than that?

FOOD FOR THOUGHT
QUESTION & ANSWER TIME

1. Are you living to satisfy the crowd, or are you living to satisfy God?

2. Do you let what others say about you sway your heart?

3. What can you do mentally and in your heart to keep your focus on pleasing God before anything else?

4

How to Approach a King – The
Art of Entertaining His Presence

In a world today where church crowds are being more entertained than ever, the art of entertaining the Presence of the Lord has nearly
been lost. The anointed ones who boldly stand
up to proclaim the holiness, beauty and greatness of our God are becoming few and far between.

Instead of rearing sons and daughters who love to entertain the Spirit of the Lord, the Church in America has raised
up a generation that adores the spotlight, fame and success.
There is nothing wrong with success, but true success is found
in what your heart is pursuing. What is it that you are choosing to promote with your life? His Presence or the praises of
men? There is no in between. Thankfully, in spite of the lack
of true worshippers in today's Church, God always has a rem-

nant, and from what I have observed that remnant is beginning to increase in strength and number.

If you want to be an entertainer of God's Presence, you must discover what really makes up the core of worship. Worship can look like a million different things (singing, painting, dancing, gift giving… etc), but the thing that makes worship what it is, is that it is something done for the purpose of touching the heart of God.

As a young boy in California I would do all sorts of things that had nothing to do with music just because I wanted to touch God's heart. I would go to our little church founded by my grandfather all alone and do different things like pick up trash, paint walls or clean bathrooms. As I would set out to do those things, with no one else watching, I would purpose in my heart that I was going to do them for the glory of the Lord. As I would pick up trash and clean I would often begin to weep because the Holy Spirit, who knew what I was doing, would come and overshadow me. Picking up trash is where I really fell in love with worshipping the Lord, not by being on a stage.

In 2014, under the direction of the Holy Spirit, I moved to Central Louisiana. I spent a little over a year on staff at a small church literally in the middle of nowhere. The year prior I was on a major tour singing with Michael W. Smith and I was doing many other things with several other well-known Christian artists. At this small church in Louisiana I was often asked to do tasks much like the ones I would do when I first fell in love with the Lord as a young boy. So I went from a lot of touring and travel, what many would call musical success, back to doing things like watering flowers, pulling weeds and vacuuming. Guess what? I absolutely loved every minute of it. You know why? Because there is no difference between worshipping God in front of thousands of people and worshipping God as you water flowers. As I would water those flowers in the 'Middle-of-Nowhere', Louisiana, I would whisper tender words to my Savior like "Lord, I love You. These are flowers that belong to Your house God, so I am going to take extra special care of them because they are Yours! I love You so much."

Entertaining the King of Kings is an art and the art begins at your core, deep within your heart. There are particular things God is looking for when He seeks out those who will worship Him: He is looking for those whose hearts are humble, those who are quick to repent. He is looking for those who are broken, those who realize their great need for God's Spirit in everything they do. These kinds of people will have lasting peace and joy. He is looking for those whose hearts are pure, those who do not want to steal anything from Him, the ones who desire to be in His glory just so they can bless Him. If any of this sounds familiar it's because I believe that much, if not all of what God is looking for in a worshipper, is what we find in the Beatitudes in Matthew chapter 5. These attributes of Christ-likeness are what we need when we come before His Presence to worship. They are the canvas upon which we paint when we bring our worship to Jesus.

The Beatitudes (NIV)

"He (Jesus) said:

"Blessed are the poor in spirit,
for theirs is the kingdom of heaven.
Blessed are those who mourn,
for they will be comforted.
Blessed are the meek,
for they will inherit the earth.
Blessed are those who hunger and thirst for righteousness,
for they will be filled.
Blessed are the merciful,
for they will be shown mercy.
Blessed are the pure in heart,
for they will see God.
Blessed are the peacemakers,

for they will be called children of God.

Blessed are those who are persecuted because of righteousness,

for theirs is the kingdom of heaven.

"Blessed are you when people insult you, persecute you and falsely say all kinds of evil against you because of me. Rejoice and be glad, because great is your reward in heaven, for in the same way they persecuted the prophets who were before you."

So let us never forget that if we approach Him humbly, we will leave honored. If we approach Him broken, we will leave healed. If we approach Him hurting, we will leave with joy. If we approach Him hungry, we will leave full. If we approach Him thirsty, we will leave quenched. If we approach Him desperate, we will leave in peace. If we approach Him bowed down low, He will lift our heads.

FOOD FOR THOUGHT
QUESTION & ANSWER TIME

1. How well do you match up with the list Jesus gave us in the Beatitudes?

2. Deep in your heart, who do you really want to impress or entertain when you are worshipping; God or man?

5

How Not to Approach a King – If You Can't Serve, Then Don't Lead

There is still a little more for me to unpack from the previous chapter. As we now know there are certain attributes that the Holy Spirit looks for when choosing His servants, the ones who will lead the charge in His Kingdom.

You do not leave your spare house keys in the hands of a stranger. In the same way God does not trust the deepest parts of who He is with a stranger.

The chapter before identified the good attributes that God desires to see in a worshipper. Now let me identify the kind of people that you want to keep as far away from your church platforms as possible. Just as God has a plan for every church, so does the enemy. The enemy will unleash spiritual attacks against churches by sending people to it who carry things that are not of God. The kinds of spirits that influence these people all have one thing in common; they seek to steal the show and then suck the life out of a church. They may do this slowly and behind the scenes or quickly from the platform, but nevertheless, that is the end goal.

Every single church at some point or another has had its struggle with a Jezebel spirit. (If you want to read more on what the spirit of Jezebel looks like read in your Bible 2 Kings chapter 9) These spirits thrive off of control, intimidation and manipulation. They slither their way to the top while living in sin and they are willing to say anything and do anything to gain more and more power.

It is a really bad sign when someone wants more power and is willing to do anything to get it. The first person to steal power through this kind of manipulation was Satan himself. Jesus never tried to selfishly take power from anyone while He was here on the Earth. Instead, even though He held all power in His hands, He chose to give His life on the cross and become the servant of all. For everything that Satan released onto the Earth, Jesus has done the opposite.

The people that the enemy sends against a church who carry a Jezebel spirit will almost always want the platform and always want the spotlight. I have never once met a person who carries a spirit like this who was thrilled about cleaning bathrooms or directing cars in the parking lot. Why? The agenda of Hell is to be served and lord over others as a dictator. On the flip side the Kingdom of Heaven's agenda is to serve. So worship teams, take an extra note here: When considering adding people to your roster, choose carefully. I advise you to choose only those who are servants and have a humble heart like Jesus. Do not let anyone onto your platform if they have a problem with serving others. For someone to desire a position on the platform without wanting to serve others is a tell tale sign that they are operating under the influence of Hell and not Heaven. Those who operate under Heaven's influence, like Christ, will always desire to serve others.

We must always remember, in the war we are fighting, our battle is not against flesh and blood. When people who are carrying something that is obviously not from God come against our churches, it is time to pray. Worship teams and leaders: Yes we need to have strategies and protocol in place to protect our churches, but we also need to know how to bring our petitions before God in prayer in these situations.

If after reading this you realize that you do, in fact, have Jezebel spirits running wild in your church, there is good news. When you take whatever action the Holy Spirit leads you to take, all you have to do is remain pure. Never forget that in 2 Kings chapter 9 it was the eunuchs that brought about the death of Jezebel, the pure virgins who had never been defiled.

Purity will always defeat perversity.

Worshippers, when we humble ourselves and keep ourselves pure before the Lord, the results can be nothing short of amazing. Positioning ourselves like this gives God permission to fight our battles and allows us to see Him more clearly than ever. *"Blessed are the pure in heart, for they will see God."* (Matthew 5:8 NIV) So let us humble ourselves, counting our brothers and sisters as better than ourselves. This is making ourselves like Jesus.

As we make ourselves more like Jesus, it will become easier and easier to spot who has not. And as we make ourselves more like Jesus, it will become easier and easier to hear and respond to the whisper of the Holy Spirit. You know, a lot of people ask me "How do you have good Spirit-led worship?" **Well, the answer is in the question. I'm not leading, the Holy Spirit is leading.** Our job as worship leaders is to position ourselves humbly like Christ. And when we do this, God will do what He does best, and bring glory to His name.

FOOD FOR THOUGHT
QUESTION & ANSWER TIME

....

1. Do you take time to serve others?

2. What does serving others look like in your day-to-day life?

3. Do you have a protocol for what is expected behaviorally for your worship team?

4. How often do you encourage your worship team to engage in serving one another and your church?

6

In the Defense of Worship

There is a serious war being waged right now against the purity of worship in America and around the world. Some of you may be aware of it already while some of you are learning about it for the first time. I want to share with you all a poetic description of what exactly is happening to worship today:

"Worship, she is a beautiful and pure virgin who carries around her neck the heart-cries of God's people. She is dressed in white as she comes before the Lord in her innocence and her brokenness. She holds in her right hand a large vessel filled with the tears of the saints and the martyrs as they have cried out 'Though You slay us Lord, we will still praise You!' Worship, she comes before God's throne day and night with her long beautiful hair and washes the feet of Jesus. She anoints them with her most precious oil and kisses them over and over again. She makes

herself completely vulnerable before her King, knowing that no matter how broken she may be, He will never turn her away. Worship is beautiful. Words cannot begin to describe how precious she is. She is sacred and holy. Worship is pure brokenness and vulnerability before the Lord.

But today in the modern American Church she is a rape victim. She has been taken from her high place at the feet of Jesus. Her hands were bound as she was drug away to be used and abused selfishly. She was molested over and over again as she was sold into prostitution. Some men saw her beauty and her virginity and lusted after her. Some men saw the glory of God upon her and said: 'Let us take her captive so that we may use her and sell her for our own profit!'

Now, here in America, she cries out, bound in her slavery, as tears flow down her face, 'When will God's people return to their first love again? When will they remember me? When will they long to kiss the feet of Jesus again? When will they weep again warm tears before the Lord longing for nothing more than to touch His heart?'"

The poetic picture you just read is the main reason why I wrote this book. The enemy has come to steal worship. He has come to kill worship and he has come to destroy worship. He must be stopped. He knows how much God loves worship and how precious it is to Him, so naturally he (Satan) wants to prostitute it in order to lessen its value.

Am I saying that it is wrong to make a living if you are a worship leader? Not at all, it's clearly not wrong. In fact, according to the scriptures when Nehemiah returned to Jerusalem to rebuild its walls the Levites (the worship leaders of the Old Testament) were not being paid as they should have been to minister before the Lord in the Temple. (Nehemiah 13) Because of this they all had to take regular day jobs out in the fields to meet their needs. Nehemiah was not happy about this and when he finally restored proper pay to the worship leaders, praises once again filled the Temple like they were supposed to.

I have a big heart for the Christian music industry. Many of my friends are a part of it and so am I. This next part is written to all of us who are involved in the Christian music industry. The real key to keeping worship from becoming perverted, lies in answering this one question: How do you view worship? Do you view it as an opportunity to bless and touch the heart of God, or do you view it as an opportunity to advance your own name? Keeping worship pure is not about who's making money and who's not, it's about who's coming to God with a pure heart and who's not. If we view working in the Christian music industry as an opportunity to advance ourselves then the way we are working is no different from the rest of the world. The work we do might as well be labeled as secular, and not something centered around Christ. This is why Paul wrote: *"Therefore judge nothing (no one's ministry) before the appointed time; wait until the Lord comes. He will bring to light what is hidden in darkness and will expose the motives of the heart. At that time each will receive their praise from God.*" (1 Corinthians 4:5 NIV)

As a Christian music industry worker, you must be very careful to not taint the purity of worship. Do not ever look at it as something that can simply be bottled up and sold for an income or else you will get on God's bad side really fast. We ought to always view worship as a precious and sacred gift that is for Jesus, our Redeemer. It was never intended to be people pleasing, only God pleasing. Therefore, the primary filter we should use when listening for what songs we will sing or promote is "Does this song please God and touch His heart?" not "Will this please the crowds?"

Imagine this with me. Say we travelled back in time, and suddenly we were there watching the woman who washed Jesus's feet with her hair. As we stand and watch her we can hear her crying. We can see how she refused to lift her head as she bowed before Jesus, and then we can see her break open her box before Him and begin to wash His feet over and over again. Then, without warning in the middle of her precious offering, a Christian industry worker interrupts and says: "Uhhh... Ma'am... We really would like to commercialize this and sell it... But frankly you're not worshipping the way that we feel would be the most marketable, and we know that you used to be an aldulterer…So we are going to need you to worship like this…" How do you think Jesus would react to that person who interrupted her? Or imagine the same thing happening to David: "Uhhh… Excuse me sir… We know you have had tremendous success with Goliath and written some hit songs… But now you are dancing before the Lord so much that your clothes are falling off? We are going to have to ask you to try something else that's a little more marketable… Maybe try hopping up and down lightly with your harp instead." How do you think God would react to that Christian industry worker's statement to David?

We cannot twist or manipulate someone's precious gifts they are giving to God so that they become something we can sell. That is what the world calls prostitution. The only acts of worship that stand out in the Bible are the undefiled and costly ones. The only acts of worship that stand out in the Bible are the ones that caused people to lose their dignity. The only acts of worship that stand out in the Bible are the ones that could have never been appealing to popular culture. They were literally untouchable by the secular world. Why? Because that's what God wants. He wants something that no one has ever given to Him or anyone else before. He wants something that's precious, something that's costly and unique. Something that someone has been saving up just for Him. That is the kind of worship that touches His heart.

There are many men and women who carry a powerful anointing when they lead worship, but not all of them are using it for the right reason. Only God can see who is really perverting worship and who isn't, who is prostituting their gifts and callings and who isn't. Although it is difficult to see the secret motives of the hearts of others, what we **can** see and examine are the motives of our own hearts. This book is not intended to be ammunition for you to shoot others down. It is intended to be ammunition for you to shoot anything down you may find in your own heart that does not please the Lord.

When we worship, amazing things happen. Satan wants to halt our worship. He wants to keep every one of these things from happening. We, as the Body of Christ can't let him get away with this. It's time to examine our hearts so that we may identify what may not be pleasing to God. When we know that our own personal worship has been made pure, this same purity will naturally pour out on others around us.

QUESTION & ANSWER TIME

1. What are some ways that the worship at your church can be cheapened?

2. How can you personally protect, defend and even restore purity back to worship?

3. If you are a paid worship leader, do you have a plan for what you would do with any excess financial blessing if God were to give it to you? Often, in order for God to give us something amazing, we need to have a plan for what we would do with it already in place.

7

cose

The Two Most Deadly Strategies Against Worship Teams

Defending the purity of worship can best be done in your church by keeping Satan's strategic tricks as far away from your team as possible. After the last chapter, it would only make sense for me to identify the two most common attacks the enemy uses against any worship team.

For generations Satan has always used the same old methods against the Body of Christ. Why? Because they work. If Satan's methods, those he used over and over again, did not work, or stopped working, then he would probably change them. Since they **do** work, he has no reason to change what he has been doing. Here are the two most common attacks against worship teams and how to overcome them:

Strategy 1 - Pride

Satan will send assignments against you to hurt your pride because he wants to wound your soul and cause you to stop worshipping. His long-term plan in doing this is to cause you to quit following Christ altogether. Here are some examples: You are a background singer, and you didn't get to lead the song that you really wanted to lead on Sunday because someone else did. Or, you are a drummer, and there happens to be another drummer that is a little better than you. Instead of you, the other drummer was asked to play drums on Sunday.

What difference does it make to God if you are worshipping Him from the platform where everyone can see you or from the back of the room where no one can see you? The solution to pride is for you to totally let go of your need to have a position or a title. If you did not need a position, or a title, then you simply would not care if someone else got the part you wanted. Pride only has a hold of you if you have a strong desire for meeting your emotional and security needs by your own strength. You must allow your emotional and security needs to be met by Jesus alone. If you do not allow Jesus to meet these needs, trust me, your problem with pride will only get much worse. Getting that position you need to make yourself feel better will not fix your problems at all. Soon you will just need something new to keep on filling the hole in your heart that only Jesus can fill. As blessed as he was, David did not trust in anything for security, except for God, and we ought to do the same. *"I will say of the Lord 'He is my refuge and my fortress, my God, in whom I trust.'"* (Psalm 91:2 NIV)

Strategy 2 - Imaginations

Most musicians and singers are naturally creative people, therefore they have powerful imaginations. The imagination can be an amazing tool for the Kingdom, or a deadly weapon in the hands of Satan. Imaginations are basically the birthing rooms of everything we do in life. Pure imaginations, partnered with the Word of God, can lead to amazing things, like new worship songs, new albums, worship centers and houses of prayer. Imaginations apart from the Holy Spirit lead to horrible things, like addictions to pornography, drugs and alcohol, extramarital affairs, and other perverted things. Worship teams, watch closely over your imaginations. Since you all have such creative minds, this can be your greatest blessing or your greatest curse.

The solution to guarding our imaginations is very simple - if we know our thoughts are not pleasing to God then we need to change them so that they are. This may require weeks, or even months, of mental discipline, but it absolutely can be done with the help of the Holy Spirit. Many Christians who are saved, born again, and truly love God, have horrible thought lives. It is because there are very few teachers who venture into instructing the Body of Christ on this area of pleasing God. Many people in the modern day Church actually believe that as long as they've got it together on the outside that "anything goes" in their thought life.

In Matthew 15 Jesus spoke sternly to the Pharisees about this very subject. Jesus clearly said that He would rather have an outward mess before an inward mess. So before you dress your best for church on Sunday morning have you dressed up your mind for it's best? You are selling yourself short if you have combed your hair perfectly but have forgotten to comb through the thoughts of your mind to make sure that they are pleasing too.

Worshippers! It is so important that we purify our imaginations. No one has an affair without imagining it first. No one declares himself, or herself, to be a homosexual without imagining it first. No one causes a church split without imagining it first. On the flip side, no one has ever healed someone in the name of Jesus without imagining it first. No one has ever started a church that reaches thousands without imagining it first. No one has ever raised someone from the dead without imagining it first. Everything that ever happens begins with a thought. The power held within our imaginations is limitless. This is why Jesus said in Matthew 5: *"You have heard that it was said, 'YOU SHALL NOT COMMIT ADULTERY'; but I say to you that everyone who looks at a woman with lust for her has already committed adultery with her in his heart."* (Matthew 5:27-28 ESV)

In the Church there are many who suffer from having an impure imagination. The good news it that there is no such thing as a thought life that is so bad that it cannot be changed. As I said earlier, it may take weeks or even months of putting the Word of God into your mind for a total change to occur, but trust me, eventually the tide will turn. The power of the name of Jesus and the power of His Word can completely cleanse and renew any dirty thought life. His Word tells us to *"Be transformed by the renewing of your mind."* (Romans 12:2 NIV) Almost every Christian knows this verse but very few actually put it into practice. When we renew our imaginations, the Word of God promises that we will be transformed. If you make up your mind to put this verse into practice and develop new thinking habits, I promise, your life will be radically changed.

It is an undeniable fact, when we read God's word, it fills us with Truth, and the Truth is what brings us freedom. Another added blessing to this is that when we have God's word hidden in our hearts, it makes it very easy for us to see which thoughts are from God and which ones are not. Worshippers – let's worship God with the very thoughts that we think. Let's have our minds made up that we will think thoughts that are pleasing to God.

FOOD FOR THOUGHT
QUESTION & ANSWER TIME

1. Do I have pride lurking in my heart? Are all of my emotional and security needs completely met by Jesus?

2. Is my imagination pure? If not, what kind of daily plan can I implement, partnered with the Word of God, to attack this problem head on and conquer it?

3. Do I have healthy spiritual leadership in my life with whom I can share everything?

8

A New Heart & Mind for God's Glory

If we want to be excellent defenders of the purity of worship, we must become defenders of our minds and spiritual territory. As we press forward for the Kingdom of God, there will be many counterattacks and retaliations from the enemy.

Worshippers, you have found the safest place you can find, if every single thought you think brings glory to the name of the Lord. How do you accomplish this? By learning to control your mind.

As I said in the last chapter, every decision you will make in your life begins with a thought in your head. The meditation of your mind controls much of how you react to the circumstances of life, and it even determines who you will become. *"As he thinks in his heart, so is he."* (Proverbs 23:7 NKJV)

Charles Spurgeon once said something that I often remind myself of: "Remember that thought is speech before God." What a powerful and convicting statement! As every person already knows, it is so easy to be seen doing the right thing on the outside, while your heart and mind are doing some stinking thinking. The real battle to bringing God glory in everything we do really does begin, and end, with what's happening on the inside of us.

Worship leaders and musicians, as we all should know, the fruit of the Holy Spirit is love, joy, peace, patience, kindness, goodness, faithfulness, gentleness, and self-control. If the Holy Spirit lives and dwells inside of you, then where is the first place love, joy, peace, patience, kindness, goodness, faithfulness, gentleness, and self-control should be happening? That's right - on the inside!

Jesus rebuked those who did everything right on the outside, but were inwardly dirty, for one simple reason: All they ever did was a lie. If inwardly our hearts' thoughts are saying: "I'm dirty! I'm unclean!" but outwardly our actions are saying: "I'm pure! I'm clean!" we are lying to ourselves. What this means is that Satan, the father of all lies, is really the father of what we are doing, and not God.

It may seem like a daunting task to conquer the realm of your heart's meditation...and let me start by saying, it absolutely is daunting. You see, this is where the hope of the cross of Jesus Christ comes into play - **You do not realize the preciousness of the blood of Jesus until you see just how badly you have need of it.** We could never attain a redeemed mind and a redeemed heart by our own human ability. Only by God's mercy can we be cleansed from our old patterns of thinking. When we have this realization, we have taken the first step to bringing God glory in everything we do. Here are some more in depth steps to gaining and keeping control over your mind:

Step 1 - Gain Control Over Your Mind

"Rejoice in the Lord always. I will say it again: Rejoice! Let your gentleness be evident to all. The Lord is near. Do not be anxious about anything, but in every situation, by prayer and petition, with thanksgiving, present your requests to God. And the peace of God, which transcends all understanding, will guard your hearts and your minds in Christ Jesus." (Philippians 4:4-6 NIV)

If we want to gain control of our minds, we must first rejoice in the Lord, and then pray about anything that may be on our minds. Why do we rejoice? Because, if God is on our side, everything really is going to be okay. We always have the promise of Heaven ahead of us if we belong to Jesus. Then, as we rejoice, we literally release and give to Christ the mental burdens we carry. We mix in with this process thanksgiving, which causes us to recall the goodness of God. It is also important that we have faith that God is actually going to bring the change to our thought life that we are hoping for. When we do this, we then have peace, because we know that God, who is a good Father, has heard us and is taking care of us.

Step 2 - Keep Control Over Your Mind

"Finally, brothers and sisters, whatever is true, whatever is noble, whatever is right, whatever is pure, whatever is lovely, whatever is admirable—if anything is excellent or praiseworthy—think about such things. Whatever you have learned or received or heard from me, or seen in me—put it into practice. And the God of peace will be with you." (Philippians 4:7-9 NIV)

Step one shows us how to gain, or regain, control over our minds. Once we have done this we are then called to dwell on whatever thoughts are praise worthy. Praise worthy thoughts are thoughts that are worthy of praise. As we do this and form new mental habits, our thought life will turn from bad to good. New thinking patterns, that are in line with the Word of God, will bring major breakthrough for anyone willing to give it a try.

Step 3 - Resist Thoughts Not From God

"We demolish arguments and every pretension that sets itself up against the knowledge of God, and we take captive every thought to make it obedient to Christ." (2 Corinthians 10:5 NIV)

Once we have begun to form new thought patterns, we can be sure the Devil will come again and try to break back in. Do you have a mental prisoner of war camp set up outside of your mind for thoughts that are not from the Lord? Every one of the verses I have used in this chapter were written by the Apostle Paul. Before his encounter with Jesus on the road to Damascus, Paul was a man who lived to murder Christians, and those he did not murder, he tortured and had imprisoned. None of the early Church leaders would have been more susceptible to mental anguish than Paul. So if there is one person that we want to learn from on the subject of controlling the mind, it is Paul. His transformation gives great hope to anyone, from any walk of life. God is able to take anyone's heart and mind and make them new by the power of His Presence. And once the Lord has done this work, *"we (continue to) take captive every thought to make it obedient to Christ."* (2 Corinthians 10:5 NIV)

FOOD FOR THOUGHT
QUESTION & ANSWER TIME

1. Do I really believe that God is able to take my mental burdens upon Himself as I lift them up in prayer?

2. Do I treat my thought life as if God is listening to every thought I think?

3. How many times do I pray each day? Do I take every one of my petitions to God and ask Him to rule over them?

9

* e n e*

The Modern-Day Basics of Running and Operating a Worship Team - Part 1

Much of this book so far has been addressing the matters of the heart. It is so important to have your heart in line, before anything else, when it is time to worship. There is absolutely no point in singing outwardly, if your heart is not singing inwardly to the Lord first.

I tell worship teams all the time that being successful in the big things is always directly linked to what you are doing with the small things. Consistency and dedication to the purity of your heart first, and then to musical excellence second, is always a recipe for success.

How blessed it is when a worship team has both a fragrance of worship that is pleasing to the Lord and an excellence in musical skill. I would like to share with you in this chapter some practical tools that will help you with the week in and week out operation of your worship team. There are several small things I have learned over the years that I consider essential for running and maintaining a healthy worship team. Lets take a look at a few of these things:

1. When choosing songs choose the ones that move your heart. I will never forget the first time one of my pastors, Lindell Cooley, took me out on the road to lead worship with him. We were playing at a big event and there were lots of people who had come out that night to worship with us. I was a little nervous before we started playing, so I asked him something like this: "Hey Pastor, what songs should I lead? I was thinking this song would go well here cause it's in this key, and the people really respond well to this particular song when I sing it…" Pastor Lindell just looked at me and said: "Phil, lead whatever is moving your heart towards the Lord. If it's not moving you towards Jesus, then how is it going to move the audience towards Jesus?" That was one of the most practical and real responses I have ever heard about song selection. It has now become a core part of my thought process when I am selecting songs to lead. When we choose the songs that are moving us as leaders into a place of deeper worship, it becomes much easier for us to take the entire church body along with us.

2. Worship leaders, when choosing songs choose the ones that you are comfortable playing and leading. You first need to choose songs based on what God is leading you to do in your heart, but to counterbalance this, you must also make sure that you are choosing songs you are actually comfortable with leading and playing. If you grew up driving a car with an automatic transmission, you would look very silly trying to jump in and drive someone else's car with a manual transmission without first being well rehearsed. Choose songs that you are familiar with and can play well, songs you know you can drive with confidence. If you are not choosing songs that you are confident with, then the chances for a Sunday morning train-wreck increase drastically.

3. Worship leaders, especially younger leaders, do not close your eyes too much when you are leading worship. You don't close your eyes when you're driving a car, or else you will become directionless. Similarly, if you close your eyes while leading worship, you will lose sight of your congregation and become directionless. Second to hearing from God, seeing what the Holy Spirit is doing in your congregation is the best compass you have when leading worship. Having Spirit-led worship actually requires that you follow the Holy Spirit. I am not saying you should never have times when you lose yourself in God's presence. There must be a fine balance between the time when you, as a leader during a service, are locked in with God and the time you are leading the church body to that place where you are. Eye contact during worship is an important part of that. A servant can not serve someone with his or her eyes closed.

4. Have a weekly practice time where your band can get together and rehearse new songs. This one might sound very basic, but I am surprised at how many worship teams actually do not do this. It can only help if you get together during the week to work on new material with your entire group. I recommend that whenever you meet, that you try learning a new song, and then brush over the others you will be playing for your services that week.

5. Within a worship team there is no such thing as over-communication. Always over-communicate the details of times, schedules and special events. So many problems can be avoided by having plenty of clear communication amongst your team. Music directors and worship leaders, you must always be sure to send everyone on your team (including sound and lyric staff) a copy of every new song (mp3's, CD's) and the corresponding chord chart, well in advance before practicing them.

6. "Without faith it is impossible to please God." (Hebrews 11:6 NIV) If I do not have faith applied to my worship, then is my worship pleasing to God? Faith affects every area of our walk with God. If we do not have faith to prophecy, then how can we prophesy? If we do not have faith to reach the lost, then how can we be a witness? If we do not have faith in the blood of Jesus, then how can we ever leave our old ways of sin behind? The same is true for worship. If we do not have faith that our worship is actually going to touch the heart of God, then will it? Worshippers, faith-less worship is not pleasing to the Lord. When you show up to worship, don't forget to mix faith in with your worship. Faith is held within your heart and applying it to your worship means you are applying your heart to worship. As you worship, let your heart imagine things like God stooping down to hear your praises. Assure yourself that His heart really is being moved by what you are singing. As you do things like this you will see a new boldness come upon your worship. *"Without faith it is impossible to please God."* (Hebrews 11:6 NIV)

FOOD FOR THOUGHT
QUESTION & ANSWER TIME

1. Does your worship team lean more heavily to choose songs based on what you are feeling in your hearts, or more towards what you all do well musically? Do you have a healthy balance of both?

2. Worship leaders, when you're leading, what percentage of the time do you have your eyes closed? Do you feel confident to lead the congregation in worship?

3. Does your worship team have excellent communication?

10

Yes, You Have What It Takes To Touch God's Heart

When we behold even just a tiny bit of such an amazing King, it is hard to imagine that we have anything to offer Him at all. When we come aching to bring Him something that's of worth, we quickly realize that even all the best this world has to offer falls short of what we know we should give Him. Just like David figured out, we **do** have something precious that we can offer God - our worship.

We do not have to be found empty handed when coming before the Lord to adore Him. Like the wise men that brought their precious gifts to the newborn King Jesus, we too can bring precious gifts to Him. Do you have hands? Then lift them to Him while they still can be raised. Do you have a voice? Then lift it to Him while you still can speak. Do you have a mind? Then change your thoughts so that every single one of them can bring Him praise. Do you have a heart? Then give it to Jesus while it is still beating.

Many struggle to truly offer the gifts they carry in worship because of one thing: Failure to focus on Jesus. Failing to focus on Jesus is truly one of the greatest, if not the greatest inhibitor of worship. **The only thing our worship is waiting on is for us to focus in and behold the beauty of God.** When we behold the beauty of God, everything else follows suit and begins to worship.

I heard a good friend of mine say something once that I will never forget: **"The amazing thing about Jesus is that His hand is attached to His heart. No one ever caused Jesus's hand to move because they won a theological argument with Him. His hand doesn't move when you touch His mind, His hand only moves when you touch His heart."** –Andres Bisonni.

When we touch God's heart in a big way, He will make sure to touch ours back in an even bigger way. Here is an example of how God did this: God did honor Solomon's name by allowing him to build an earthly Temple. It was a place of splendor, and yes the Lord did come to rest there. But God **Himself** built an even greater temple to honor the name of David - the Temple of His son Jesus "The Son of David."

Jesus was not called the "The Son of David" by accident. God honored David's name and attached it to His own Son because David was a man who touched His heart in such a big way. So how can you touch God's heart? Have you made touching His heart your life's mission? Those that set out to live their lives to touch God's heart will always be the most blessed and happy people.

FOOD FOR THOUGHT
QUESTION & ANSWER TIME

1. When is the last time you did something for the Lord's honor? When is the last time you came into a worship setting with the mindset that it was a time set apart for you to devote all that you are to Him?

2. Do you see your very body as an instrument of worship? Do you view it as a temple for the Holy Spirit?

3. As a Christian, how much time do you spend doing things to touch God's heart?

11

Nobody Touches God's Heart Accidentally

Nobody touches God's heart accidentally. Just think about that for a moment. God's heart has never been touched unintentionally. It is only touched by those who yearn to touch it, and it is only won by those yearn to win it. God's heart feels far more than any human's ever will, and his emotions are far deeper than any of ours will ever be. If His heart feels and has emotions, and can be won, similarly to how a person's can be won, it is important that we ask ourselves what it is that actually moves His heart.

A great starting point on this topic is King David. David was a man after God's own heart and his thoughts were continually fixed on the Lord. It is easy for us to see through the scriptures that David was always thinking about ways to intentionally do things for God. The birthing room of worship is that place in your heart where you seek out ways to intentionally touch God's heart.

In 1 Chronicles 17 there is a written record of an exchange that happens between King David and the Lord that I believe is one of the most significant acts of worship ever. If only there could be many more like David who want to worship the Lord like this!

After David was settled in his palace, he said to Nathan the prophet, "Here I am, living in a house of cedar, while the ark of the covenant of the Lord is under a tent." Nathan replied to David, "Whatever you have in mind, do it, for God is with you."

But that night the word of God came to Nathan, saying: "Go and tell my servant David, 'This is what the Lord says: You are not the one to build me a house to dwell in. I have not dwelt in a house from the day I brought Israel up out of Egypt to this day. I have moved from one tent site to another, from one dwelling place to another. Wherever I have moved with all the Israelites, did I ever say to any of their leaders whom I commanded to shepherd my people, "Why have you not built me a house of cedar?"' "Now then, tell my servant David, 'This is what the Lord Almighty says: I took you from the pasture, from tending the flock, and appointed you ruler over my people Israel. I have been with you wherever you have gone, and I have cut off all your enemies from before you. Now I will make your name like the names of the greatest men on earth. And

I will provide a place for my people Israel and will plant them so that they can have a home of their own and no longer be disturbed. Wicked people will not oppress them anymore, as they did at the beginning and have done ever since the time I appointed leaders over my people Israel. I will also subdue all your enemies.

"'I declare to you that the Lord will build a house for you: When your days are over and you go to be with your ancestors, I will raise up your offspring to succeed you, one of your own sons, and I will establish his kingdom. He is the one who will build a house for me, and I will establish his throne forever. I will be his father, and he will be my son. I will never take my love away from him, as I took it away from your predecessor. I will set him over my house and my kingdom forever; his throne will be established forever.'" Nathan reported to David all the words of this entire revelation. (1 Chronicles 17:1-15 NIV)

What I love most in this section of scripture is when the Lord says to David: *"Wherever I have moved with all the Israelites, did I ever say to any of their leaders whom I commanded to shepherd my people, 'Why have you not built me a house of cedar?'"* This implies and indicates that David was thinking of ways, above and beyond, to touch God's heart. To David just continuing to do for God what had always been done wasn't good enough. I have to say it again: **Thinking of how you can bless God and touch His heart is the birthing room of worship.** David fixed his eyes and his heart completely on God and was always thinking of ways to go further and deeper with his worship. This is the reason he was one of the greatest worshippers in history. *"I have set the Lord always before me, and because He is at my right hand I will not be moved."* (Psalm 16:8 KJV)

I would like to get a little interactive with this chapter by asking you this question: What is it that you can personally do, to go above and beyond, to touch God's heart? I want to encourage you to come up with your own unique ways to bless God's heart. Here are some great ideas to help get you started:

1. Do you have money? Set aside more than what you would regularly tithe and offer it to God. The amount you decide to give is completely up to you. This action begins by purposing in your heart that you want to bless the Lord with what you have by doing something for him that is above and beyond. You can always give directly to the Church, as the Church is the very Bride of Christ. Every husband knows that if his wife is happy he will be happy. If you go above and beyond to take care of Christ's Bride, He will return the favor many times over. You can also purpose in your heart to financially bless someone who is in need. Remember what Jesus said: *"The King will reply, 'Truly I tell you, whatever you did for one of the least of these brothers and sisters of mine, you did for me.'"*

(Matthew 25:40 NIV) When we give to those in need, we are giving straight to Jesus.

2. Write down the meditation of your heart to the Lord. Men, this might seem weird to you, but if David the giant-slayer did it, you can do it. Take time to sit before the Lord and think about Him. Begin to think about what you are thankful for. Maybe you are thankful for how He has changed your life, or how He has brought you through many things. Or, maybe you are in a rough spot at the moment. Either way sit down before the Lord and write out your heart to Him.

Be honest with God and tell Him how you really feel. If you are broken, you can run to God and pour that out before Him. If you have a family member that is lost, or not doing so well, you can pour that out before Him too. David was always pouring out his soul's cry before the Lord like water. As you empty your soul before God like this, you will find that He will respond to you and a release will come upon you that might actually trigger a deep emotional healing. You may also find as you pour your heart out the Holy Spirit will come alongside you and help bear your burdens. This kind of writing, that is honest and sincere unto the Lord, is very inviting to the Holy Spirit.

As you do this over time, I would encourage you to keep a journal, maybe start writing poetry, or even try writing songs. Make sure to keep these things you share with God stored up somewhere for remembrance. Aren't we all thankful that David saved some of his Psalms for us to read all these thousands of years later? Here is an example of something I personally wrote to the Lord one day:

> I'm so lost without You Lord. I am so helpless without You Jesus.
>
> There is no getting around the fact that I need you every single hour of my life.
>
> Like how an infant weeps when they lose sight of their father so I am with you.
>
> To lose sight of you for even a moment is unbearable.
>
> All that I have in life is You Lord. What else do I have to hold onto?
>
> Nothing else will be there for forever like You will be.
>
> Without Your Presence God I cannot sleep.
>
> Without Your Presence I cannot think and I have no peace.
>
> Lord, please let me be found in You.
>
> I know I do not own any costly oil for Your feet, but I do have my tears.

To see Your faithful love for me is a wonder in and of itself.

How, when You are seated so high in Heaven and enthroned in glory, are you aware of me?

How do You love me so deeply? You take note of every thought I think.

You always do special things just to show me how much You love me.

You know the things no one else could possibly know I am thinking.

Regardless of all my past mistakes You still show me eternal affection.

There truly is no one else like you God!

Father, give me eyes to see only You.

Give me a renewed mind that has no choice but to dwell on Your goodness.

Let my very thoughts be worship unto You.

Let every thought I think give You praise!

This truly is my heart's desire - To never be found not worshipping You!

Give me new strength that I will dedicate to loving You.

Give me a new heart. Purify it and make me clean.

Give this to me, not so I can use it for selfish reasons

– Only give it to me so that I may worship You!

Your presence alone satisfies me.

Your presence is the only thing in life that truly refreshes me.

So let it be known among the whole Earth that there is nothing more I desire than Jesus.

No place is my home but You Lord.

No person is my fulfillment but You Lord.

And no person is my strength except for You Lord.

3. Those who are married can relate to this: Say you and your spouse have a special song together, or maybe you have even written a song for your spouse. Imagine what they would feel when they got home from a long day at work and they heard that song playing in the house. Your spouse would automatically know that you had been thinking about them. Now that's pretty romantic. Why not do those same kinds of things for God? When you leave your house, put on some music that will entertain the Lord. God's presence shows up where He is lifted up. It will really touch His heart to see you doing that for Him, and it will also bless you when you get home and sense His presence lingering.

Go ahead and let your mind venture off into more ways

of how you can touch God's heart. Continuing to do what you have always done on Sunday mornings is not going above and beyond. What can you do that is extra special for Him? What can you do that is unseen, or maybe even a sacrifice? Remember, no one has ever touched God's heart without intending to do so. Let's be intentional.

FOOD FOR THOUGHT
QUESTION & ANSWER TIME

1. What are some new things you can do to intentionally touch God's heart?

2. How often do you think of different ways you can touch God's heart? Daily? Weekly? Monthly? Yearly?

3. What do you think would happen to your relationship with Jesus, if you thought of new ways to touch His heart, daily?

12

Worship and Thankfulness

Many things can hinder the manifestation of the Presence of God during worship in a church when we overlook an essential ingredient; thanksgiving.

A great key to properly entering into the Presence of the Lord lies in what David wrote long ago: *"Enter his gates with thanksgiving and his courts with praise; give thanks to him and praise his name."* (Psalm 100:4 NIV) David absolutely hit the nail on the head when he wrote this. Thanksgiving is the premiere gateway when it comes to entering into the place of praising God. Why? It is impossible for someone to be thankful without remembering. You cannot tell someone 'thank you' without observing the reason *why* you are thanking them.

When you come to God with thanksgiving in your heart it causes you to recall all of the good things He has done for you. Having these things at the forefront of your mind is what you need most if you really want to praise the Lord.

It is no wonder why thankfulness is such a huge key in worship. It unlocks the place in our hearts where the good things that God has done for us are tucked away for safekeeping and remembrance. Unlocking this place will cause exuberance and joy to burst out from the innermost part of our being. If you ever wonder why some people are edgy worshippers, why they like to dance or shout aloud when they're praising God, it's probably because they have a real reason to worship. They have a real reason to be thankful. When we thankfully remember everything God has done for us, how can we not dance or shout aloud? We get to worship God for real reasons. We get to praise Him for the real things He has done just for us.

FOOD FOR THOUGHT
QUESTION & ANSWER TIME

1. When you are leading worship do you recall all the good things that God has done for you?

2. Does your church lack joy in times of worship? If so, why do you think that is? Could it possibly be linked to a lack of being thankful?

3. What could you do to encourage a culture of thankfulness in your church body?

13

case

Our Ministries Belong On the Altar at All Times

As we become more accomplished as defenders of the purity of worship, we must always keep a clear focus on the realm in which we function. This is to guard against becoming distracted by the great authority, or high position, Christ may give us.

We have each been called to serve as Kings and Priests unto the Lord. As we do this, we must never forget that the Kingdom we serve is not our own, but our Fathers. The King of Kings and Lord of Lords, Jesus, did not even claim the Kingdom to be His own. This is why He said: *"Yours is the Kingdom…"* (Matthew 6:13) He, being God's Son, acknowledged His place in relation to His Father. Then, His Father, to whom the Kingdom does belong, exalted Him to the highest place of honor as King of Kings and Lord of Lords.

So why then are there ministers and servants of the Lord who treat their assigned ministries, within God's Kingdom, as if they have total ownership over them? If the Kingdom at large does not belong to us, then what makes us think the smaller ministries and functions would belong to us?

Imagine this for a moment: Say there was an absolute monarchy that had a good King as it's royal ruler. This good King was at war with an evil kingdom. Within the absolute monarchy there were many different ministries that were all functioning to serve the greater good of the kingdom as a whole. One of these ministries was the ministry of defense. The ministry of defense existed to implement whatever military policies the good King knew would be necessary for the protection of His people. One day the man who the King had placed as head of the ministry of defense became impatient and began to take military action without the consent of the King. What do you think this good King did when he found out about the rebellious leader's actions? He removed him with expedience and had him thrown into prison, because his actions were that of defiance and treason.

So, what are leaders in the church thinking when they get into the mindset that they get to run their own ministry without consulting the head of the Kingdom first? Worship leaders, singers, musicians and other ministers; if you operate your ministry and make decisions without consulting the King (who is the Word of God) first, is your ministry a legitimate ministry? I'm going to be very frank with you. Whenever God gives us an anointing, or a ministry, we do not have the right to do whatever we want with it. Any anointing or ministry exists to serve the greater good of the Kingdom of Heaven, and Jesus Christ is Head of the Kingdom.

If the head of the ministry of defense did whatever they wanted with their resources, it would no longer be considered a legal ministry. It would be considered rogue and would quickly be shut down. Within God's Kingdom it is no different. I have never once heard of, or seen, a ministry in His Kingdom that went rogue that He did not humble severely or take away it's legitimacy.

Now, is God patient? Yes. Does He pardon and forgive far more than any earthly king? Yes. But why go there in the first place? Why venture into the danger zone with God when you could just do things right the first time? We who are in ministries, and especially those who are heads of ministries, must know exactly how to avoid this danger.

The safest way to make sure that God does not catch any of us in a rogue mindset and take action against our ministry, is to keep our ministry on the Altar of the Lord at all times. God's altar is the place of sacrifice where only holy things are placed and the ministries within His Kingdom are most certainly holy. Your ministry is something that must always be laid out in a position of vulnerability before the Lord (who is the Word of God). Even if your ministry is world-renowned and having global impact, you must still keep it upon the altar and hold it with a loose grip. You must always remember that your ministry does not exist to serve you, but it exists to serve Him. Always remembering exactly who it is you are working for will always cause you to keep the right perspective.

Worshippers, we have to get this right, because this is exactly where Satan failed. Just how the good King in my story would remove a rebellious head of a ministry from His kingdom is how God removed Satan from His Kingdom long ago. Satan was the first to be exiled from God's goodness because He thought his ministry was all about him. Therefore, I propose that we must do the exact opposite of Satan and always remember that our ministries are not all about us, but all about Jesus.

I will talk some more about the Altar of the Lord and what this means for us today in the next chapter, but for now let me tell you a little secret: The Altar of the Lord, the place where we ought to always keep our ministries, is the only place in the Bible where the Fire of God is legally allowed to burn. Assuredly I say to you that if you keep your ministry upon the altar, then the Fire of God will never depart from it.

FOOD FOR THOUGHT
Question & Answer Time

1. Have I looked at my ministry lately, as something that is for my own gain and not for serving Jesus?

2. How do I make sure that I do not take my ministry off the Altar of the Lord and put it under my own control?

3. Is there any better place for my life's work than in God's hands and under His direction?

4. How important is prayer and knowing God's Word when it comes to operating my ministry?

14

How to Start & Maintain a Fire
in Your Heart for Worship

" "T"he fire on the altar shall be kept burning on it;
it shall not go out. The priest shall burn wood
on it every morning, and he shall arrange the burnt offering on it and shall burn on it the fat of the peace offerings. Fire shall be kept burning on the altar continually;
it shall not go out." (Leviticus 6:12-13 NIV)

Worship under the Law of Moses was almost always presented in the form of a sacrifice, and a sacrifice always involved something being killed. How does this apply to us
today? When we come before the Lord to worship there is
always some bit of our flesh that needs to die. There are so
many petty things that can hold us back from total surrender
in our worship and these things are better off dead.

Most of the things that can take away from our worship
occur inwardly. A common inward activity that can steal from

your worship is being too worried about what others think of you when you're worshipping. Not all extravagant worship is really pleasing to God. If we do anything in worship as a mere reaction to what others think of us when they're watching, then the ones we are really worshipping are ourselves. Always remember that worship is not for you, nor is it for those watching. It is all for the Lord. Our actions and reactions in worship should always be totally centered on Him.

Another common thing that can sneak its way even into an entire church is a loss of passion to worship. If you are no longer excited to worship God, it can only be because some part of your flesh has taken hold of the highest place in your heart. Again, these things must be put to death. We were called to deny ourselves when we decided to follow Jesus, and this includes what happens inwardly when we are worshipping.

When we worship we are keeping our flesh from having any glory. In fact, it is impossible to worship God from any fleshly perspective. If we try to do this, then our worship will be carnally driven and not Spirit driven. The quickest route to getting to the place in worship where deep calls unto deep is to leave our own problems and issues behind and focus everything we are on His beauty, His holiness, His faithfulness and His perfection.

The verse mentioned at the beginning of this chapter talked about the Fire of God that was used by the High Priest for the consuming of sacrifices. I want us to take a look at some basics keys of how a fire is built, sustained and maintained. God always asked the Levites, His set apart workers in and around His presence, to watch closely over His holy fire. He assigned them much like He has assigned us today to sustain it, maintain it and make sure it never dies.

The first step to starting a proper fire for God is that you must have the Altar swept clean every single morning. Where is the Altar of the Lord found nowadays? It is no longer found near any physical temple because God now calls us His Temple. The Altar of the Lord is now found within our hearts. Each day as you come before the Lord, sweep the altar clean and blow off the ashes of yesterday. Do not think about lighting a new fire in your heart until you have let go of yesterday's mistakes, taken care of any sin in your life, and put your soul in the proper position to freshly burn for the Lord. Once you have asked for any forgiveness where you may have needed it, you can then begin to lay upon the altar of your heart the fuel for the next day's fire. God wants the place where His fire burns inside of us to be neat and orderly.

The next step is identifying the type of fuel that you will need to use for the Fire of God. The fuel that we need, both now and forevermore, is the Word of God. We take God's promises and we fill our hearts with them. Here are some common examples of God's promises that we can throw onto the flame in our hearts. Though our circumstances may look bleak we can say: "I will live and not die and proclaim the works of the Lord!" Though our nation may seem lost in darkness we can say: "The Lord has declared that if we, His people, humble ourselves, turn from our wicked ways and seek His face, He WILL come and heal our land!" Though everything may be against us, we who are His can say: "If God be for us, who can be against us?" When we begin to put these things upon the Altar of our hearts immediately we will be reminded of the faithfulness of God and the millions of reasons we have to worship Him. As we declare the Word of God, our souls and our minds will begin to line up with the Holy Spirit. When the fuel is in the proper place to be set ablaze, we have then moved ourselves into position to receive the next step to sustaining and maintaining the fire of God.

All the steps listed so far are within our own power. They are things that we are responsible for, not the Lord. Once we have taken the initiative to fulfill the first two steps, all we need to do is wait upon the Lord. The next step must be supernatural, because the Fire of God does not come from any man, it comes straight from the throne of Jesus Christ.

John the Baptist said of Jesus: *"I baptize you with water for repentance. But after me comes one who is more powerful than I, whose sandals I am not worthy to carry. He will baptize you with the Holy Spirit and with fire.* " (Matthew 3:11 NIV) Jesus alone baptizes in God's Holy Fire. So the spark that we need to ignite true worship within our hearts can come only from His Spirit. This process of waiting on the Lord and seeking Him for this baptism of fire may take time, but if you tarry for Him, trust me, He will come. The Lord never fails to baptize those who are hungry for His Spirit and for His fire. Once this step happens the Altar of your heart is officially lit! Always continue to keep feeding your heart the fuel of the Word of God and make sure the Altar is swept clean every morning. Keep your fire alive every day! Don't let it become dampened because the ashes of yesterday are taking up the space that it needs to burn with intensity. The best way to defend the purity of worship is to continually keep your heart ablaze.

FOOD FOR THOUGHT
QUESTION & ANSWER TIME

1. Do you have the baptism of the Holy Spirit? Is this being renewed in your life? If you do not have the baptism of the Holy Spirit, when is the last time you asked for it?

2. How much time do you spend each day tending to the fire in your heart?

3. Do you take time to continually give God your heart? One of my favorite prayers to pray is "Lord Jesus, I give you my heart all over again today."

15

Do You Need a Special Anointing to Worship?

I love the anointing of God and I am so thankful for it. To be able to sense this precious gift of Heaven partnering with what He has called me to do is an incredible thing that I never want to lose.

In my few years as a worship leader I have had many people come up to me and ask me to pray for them so that they may receive a special anointing for worship. I am so honored that people would ask me this, and yes, I will pray for them. But I always make sure to tell them this as well: **God can anoint us for anything. But what are you chasing as a worshipper? Are you chasing after an anointing or after the heart of God?**

Did David worship God because he was anointed? No, that would have made no sense. David worshipped God because he loved Him with all of his heart. When it comes to worship, chasing after an anointing will not get you half as far as simply pursuing the heart of God. When we worship we should not rely on an anointing. Instead, what we should really rely on is the depths of our love and passion for God, because this is the true source of worship.

The scriptural truth I always use to back this up is the story of David. David did not wait for his time to be anointed to start chasing after the heart of God. He never had **"Anointing Day: Samuel comes to the house"** penciled in on his calendar. In fact, David probably never even expected to be anointed. According to scripture he was already a man after God's own heart long before the day Samuel showed up.

If I can be vulnerable for a minute, I would like to tell you that my life's story is similar, in a way, to David's. As I was writing this chapter, I recalled that I have never once asked God or a minister to pray for me for a special anointing to come upon me for leading worship. I really can't even pinpoint the moment I realized that I was anointed. But, what I can recall are all of the moments when I was so in love with Jesus, that it drove me to worship Him with everything I had.

I did not have much as a young boy. I couldn't play any instruments, except maybe just a few notes on the piano. I had a little raspy voice that I could lift to Jesus as I longed for

Him. All I had was my heart, and it seemed all I could offer was more and more of it to him. I had tiny little hands that I could raise to Him when I was all by myself in my bedroom. You do not need to have much to bring God an acceptable offering of worship. Mainly, all you need is your heart.

Do not wait for an anointing to come before you really start loving God. **If David had waited for a special anointing to start worshipping God he would have never been a man after God's own heart.** If you feel limited because you have never had someone pray for a special anointing to come upon you, let me just break that off right now and give you full permission to go ahead and show God just how much you love Him. Start pursuing Jesus and pour all of your heart out before Him. **If you do this and don't let up, trust me, just like David, the anointing will chase you down instead of you chasing it.**

FOOD FOR THOUGHT

QUESTION & ANSWER TIME

1. Do you chase anything else, in addition to chasing after God's heart, when you are worshipping?

2. Are there any strongholds in your mind that hold you back from worshipping God and loving Him with all you have?

3. Have you placed receiving gifts from God on a higher pedestal than just loving God for who He is?

16

The Praises of Men
Is a Deadly Poison

Worshippers, as you might have figured out by now, we were not called to do what we do for the entertainment of people. We were not called to affect the sway of worldly popularity, or gain the affection of earthly kings. No, we worship for one thing and one thing only - to touch the heart of God.

It is written in 2 Timothy that in the last days many will become lovers of themselves. In today's day and age, cameras, lights and receiving more and more social media followers has become the primary pursuit of many worship teams across America. Are lights, cameras and social media followers a bad thing? No, but if there is no genuine love for God's presence what's the point?

Do you need to look amazing, and does anyone else need to know about it, for you to worship God? Absolutely not. Some of my most powerful moments in God's presence have been away from the stage and cameras in a room alone, when no one else was watching. **When you love someone it does not matter who else knows about it, just as long as the one you love knows.**

For many, having man's approval often means more than having God's approval. The real danger of this, the praises of men, is that it actually **can** affect you. It **absolutely** can make you drunk in your heart and shift your focus away from giving everything to Jesus. When you settle in your heart that having the affirmation of man is more important than having the affirmation of God, you set yourself up to be sold short of all that God has for you.

We must make it our daily fight that nothing will take our gaze off of His beautiful face. Worshippers, we must wrestle with the nasty things within us that want to dilute the purity of our worship, until they are under total submission to the Holy Spirit. Once we have them there, we must keep them there. Whether they are from my own flesh or spiritual attacks from the enemy, I wrestle with things constantly that want to dirty the purity of my own worship. I never stop assassinating thoughts of selfish ambition and pride. John Newton, the famous writer of "Amazing Grace" once said: **"My heart is like a country but half subdued. Mutinies and insurrections are daily happening."** And isn't this the case with all of us? The Devil is always working hard to lure us into prostituting and cheapening our worship, so he can make it dirty, because he knows how beautiful and precious it is to God.

The good news is that God is shaking the Church in America at the moment, and awakening her to His presence once again. I know in my heart that a third Great Awakening is indeed going to sweep across this nation. Before it does, there is much more of this shaking that needs to happen. The shaking of God is actually a really good sign, because the only time you shake someone is when you want them to wake up from a deep sleep. God is showing us by His actions today that He still loves His church fervently and refuses to let her drift off into a deep sleep on Him.

Until this work of awakening is complete, there will be many worship teams and ministries in America that will spend far more time trying to build their fan bases and trying to look cool than they will seeking God's presence. They will know far more about starting an Instagram page and faithfully building it up than they will about prayer and building up their most holy faith. They will be far more familiar to the sounds of social media notifications than they will be with the sounds of their Shepherd's voice. Worship teams, especially worship leaders, do not fall into this dangerous trap! We do not do what we do for fame or for the exaltation of ourselves. That's the Devils modus operandi, not ours. To take worship, something that is set apart for touching God's heart, and then use it for your own gain is to pervert worship altogether.

Therefore, I commit this to you, the reader of this book: **In the last days blessed is the man who sets aside the strength of his gifting and his talent, who sets aside the amounts of money in is his pocket book to rely solely on the Holy Spirit! When men trust in God like this His Spirit moves and everything is shaken.** Worship leaders, do not settle to trust in the praises of men, or the confidence you have in your talents! Choose only to trust in the power of the Holy Spirit.

Here is an amazing story from the Bible you can follow as an example: John the Baptist had the premiere ministry of his day and possibly even the largest following before Jesus appeared on the scene. Thousands were coming to the Jordan River to see what was happening. Even the Pharisees and religious leaders were making trips out to see him. John was a radical. He dressed differently and preached with fire and zeal. To many of his followers he must have been the hip new preacher with the most cutting edge message and the mightiest anointing. But guess what? One day Jesus showed up and John's ministry suddenly disappeared. Wait a minute… Because of **Jesus** showing up John's ministry dwindled overnight? Yes.

So, was John the Baptist a failure because his ministry evaporated all of the sudden? No. He was actually an absolute success! As I paraphrase, let's look at what happened in the book of John chapter three, where we find the amazing response that John had to the disappearance of his ministry because of Jesus. John's main followers came up to him and said: "John! John! Everyone has left us. Isn't this bad? Aren't you the anointed man of God? Shouldn't we have a great following still?" John, knowing full well that his entire ministry had deserted him because of Jesus, replied to his closest disciples: *"A person can receive only what is given them from heaven. You yourselves can testify that I said, 'I am not the Messiah but am sent ahead of him.' The bride belongs to the bridegroom. The friend who attends the bridegroom waits and listens for him, and is full of joy when he hears the bridegroom's voice. That joy is mine, and it is now complete. He must become greater; I must become less."* (John 3:27-30 NIV)

In the American Church today, where ministry success equates to numbers and crowd sizes, John the Baptist would most certainly be a total misfit. Some of you reading this book right now are going to lead worship on great stages in front of thousands of people, while some of you will be **assigned by God** to go to small churches in foreign countries where social media does not even exist. Some of you will write songs with the greatest songwriters and hear them played on the radio, while some of you will write songs and the only person who will ever hear them is Jesus. Please remember that there is no difference in God's eyes between either one of these scenarios. As long as you know, without a doubt, that you are obeying God, you are being successful! We must remember the words of John the Baptist in times like today where there is such an emphasis on popularity equating to success. *"God in Heaven appoints each person's work. You know I told you that I was not the Messiah, the one to be worshipped and praised, I was just here to prepare the way for Him, that is all."* (John 3:27-28 paraphrase)

For those who will be under the spotlight, let me lend to you a warning about the great stages, fame and popularity: Many more are they that fall away who gain the affection and praises of men, because they become so easily drunk on it. Many more are they that become insecure and lonely who gain the affection and praises of men, because they so easily place their identity in it. No matter what happens during the course of your life, make up your mind to be like John the Baptist. **Make sure that nothing matters more to you than**

being obedient to God. Do not do any of what you are doing because of any other motive than to obey Him. There is rest, safety and security in knowing that you are taking each and every step in obedience. If you do this, then it won't matter to you if you have ten, or ten million listening to your latest worship album.

FOOD FOR THOUGHT
QUESTION & ANSWER TIME

1. Are you easily swayed by being popular, or by the praises of men?

2. What would you do if God asked you to take all of your worship and go "private" with it and make it for His ears only?

3. Do you know deep in your heart what your purpose is? Do you know what the work is that God has assigned to you, as well as John the Baptist did?

4. Would it make a huge difference to you if a large crowd showed up to partake in your ministry, or just a few people?

17

The Clash of Cultures
- Heaven Versus Hell -

This chapter is inspired in part by a message that I heard in Texas City, Texas, delivered by a good friend of mine, Pastor Kevin Herrin. Every born again believer knows that Earth is a great battleground. It does not take an advanced Christian to figure out that we are in a war while we are here on this side of eternity.

There are thousands of different world cultures today that carry things within them, things that do not line up with the Word of God. Every believer needs to know that when you become a Christian your culture, or former background, no longer takes precedence over the Word of God. Let me talk a little bit about the current day American culture, how it does not agree with the Word of God, and some of the dangers this entails for those who are set apart to lead worship.

America is the trendsetting nation. It is the land where the coolest things and most popular people are celebrated beyond measure. This puts worship leaders and those who are called to be warriors for the Lord in a position to sink or swim. How so? We know as worshippers that we are called to keep ourselves pure and set apart, especially if we want the anointing of God to rest upon us. So, what then do we do when the world, or even some in the church who are not mature in the Word of God ask us, whether purposely or in innocently, to entertain things that are unholy and offensive to the Holy Spirit? When popular American culture challenges the Kingdom of God within us, what do we who are called to worship do? Do we take a firm stand and refuse to compromise? Or do we give in and hand over, little by little, what the blood of Jesus won for us on Calvary?

I know I am liable to start arguments and lose friends over this, but it is more important that I tell you the Truth of God's word than keep it hidden from you. This current generation in America loves to celebrate evil. Jesus said that we are to love nothing more than God and that we are to love Him with all of our heart, mind, soul and strength. How can we possibly love God like this and celebrate evil at the same time? It is simply impossible. Worshippers, you are not called to celebrate evil, nor are you called to use it for entertainment. You are called to do the opposite. **"Abstain from every form of evil."** (1 Thessalonians 5:22 ESV)

So what do you do when pop culture gives you something like Harry Potter, something that is filled with witchcraft, sorcery, spells and curses? What do we as worshippers do then? Do we entertain it? Do we watch it? What if even your best friend who is a leader in your church owns the entire Harry Potter series and adores it? You have to know this Truth straight from the Word of God: **King Saul entertained a witch and the very next day was the day that he died.** When we are found celebrating evil, it is absolutely impossible for us to be found loving God. Those who are called and set apart for the Lord should never entertain any form of witchcraft. Some may argue that it is innocent fun and that it actually has a positive story line. To entertain anything birthed from evil is to commit spiritual adultery against Jesus. **If you hold fast to keep the celebration of witchcraft and other spirits near to you, think about the message you are sending the Holy Spirit.** Witchcraft is not a game. The dark unseen powers that the generations before us wrestled out of the Church are attempting to make their way back in through movies and entertainment.

King Saul, God's anointed one, made the mistake of entertaining witchcraft in 1 Samuel chapter 28. He chose to entertain a woman who used spells and magic. She was able to call upon spirits in the supernatural realm, just like some of the things we see in Harry Potter. When he did this, God went ahead and took the Kingdom from him. **Witchcraft and sorcery were the catalyst that accelerated the crashing down of Saul's kingdom and life. People who are aligned with the heart of Saul are the ones who are okay with compromising their allegiance to the Lord to get whatever their flesh wants.**

Now Church, answer this question: Is there any difference between entertaining witchcraft in real life and entertaining it on a television screen? In America, we miss seeing much of the damage that these things carry out, because we have become so bogged down with the distractions and cares of this life. Trust me, in poorer nations where there aren't as many distractions and cares of this life, the Church is constantly witnessing the horrors of demonic forces orchestrated by witches and illegal mediators, between here and the other side of eternity.

Do you remember Simon, the sorcerer, in the book of Acts, chapter 8? He actually wanted to be used by God. He wanted to continue the use of witchcraft by paying the disciples for the Holy Spirit. He wanted to commingle his love of sorcery with God's power. Peter looked at Simon the sorcerer and said to him: *"May your money perish with you, because you thought you could buy the gift of God with money! You have no part or share in this ministry, because your heart is not right before God. Repent of this wickedness and pray to the Lord in the hope that he may forgive you for having such a thought in your heart. For I see that you are full of bitterness and captive to sin."* (Acts 8:20-23 NIV)

Worshippers, let me just spell this out. Every single time witchcraft, spells, magic and sorcery are mentioned in the Bible, it is not good. God, under the Old Covenant, commanded that any person involved with witchcraft be put to death. *"Do not allow a sorceress to live."* (Exodus 22:18 NIV) So, why then would you watch it on a DVD in your house? Why then would you fill your house with books where spells are written out in them? Why then would you stand in line to celebrate the night of its release at a movie theater? When you stand in line to celebrate the release of a movie filled with witchcraft, think about what you are doing! You are actually gathering with others to celebrate something evil being released from Hell onto the Earth.

Instead of watching movies that are evil, why not watch something that is pure and uplifting, something that does not offend the Holy Spirit? Many Christians in America have bought into thinking that they need to be "in" with the current culture. Worshippers, please hear me out! You have to know that the world's culture is always at war with God's culture. That's just the way it is always going to be until Christ returns. Very seldom does even one nation's culture line up with Heaven's. Every time the culture of a nation does not line up with the Kingdom (which is most of the time) its mission is to send people to Hell. Its mission is to infiltrate the Church and pull Christians back under Satan's yoke and put unnecessary weight on God's children, in order to slow down the mission of Heaven.

I don't know about you, the reader of this book, but I, the writer, want to be as pure as I can before Jesus. I want to go through everything I own and make sure there is nothing in my possession that could ever upset God or go against His word. Please stay away from evil. The Bible, in the New Testament, commands us to avoid even the very appearance of evil. It even goes as far to say that it is shameful to merely talk about evil. So please don't use it for personal entertainment on your television. Worshippers, God wants you pure and He wants you holy. When you lead worship, He wants you to be the cleanest reflection of His glory possible, and mixing the world's "popular" culture with the Kingdom's is never going to help pull that off.

FOOD FOR THOUGHT
Question & Answer Time

1. What are some compromised areas in your life where you have entertained the world's culture?

2. What are some cultural things in your neighborhood, city or region that are not in line with Heaven's culture? What can you do to stand for Christ in these areas?

3. When you remove things from your life that are not pleasing to the Holy Spirit, how can you make sure they do not get back in?

18

The Modern-Day Basics
of Running and Operating
a Worship Team - Part 2

As we dig deeper into *Defending the Purity of Worship* I would like to continue to give you more practical insight to help you successfully run or be a part of a worship team. As I said in Chapter 9, having large-scale success is always directly linked to being faithful with the smaller things. It is always good to examine yourself to see what kind of habits you are building. If we pay attention, and are dedicated to what doesn't seem to be that important, we can then be trusted by God with what really seems important.

Here are some more practical steps to running and operating a worship team:

1. Musicians: Always show up to practice at least 15 minutes early. Do not use the assigned practice time to set up your gear. This is not fair to the rest of the team. Let your worship leader know that you will need to arrive early to prepare your equipment. Always be ready to play when the scheduled practice time starts.

2. Worship leaders and band directors: You will have people cancel on you last minute. Be patient and do not react in anger. However, if there is a consistent pattern of tardiness with a particular team member, I recommend taking the issue to your pastor and then having a group meeting with that person and your pastor to discuss the issue. A word of wisdom: If you are a leader, never ever bring correction to anyone on the worship team without running it by and involving your pastor. When you involve the head of your church or another higher up with correction, the conversation you have will carry much more weight.

3. Set up a standard period of time for all new potential band members to show faithfulness before they can join the group. The amount of time you decide on is up to you. Again, I recommend involving your pastor in this process so that it is blessed. Pastors have been given a special assignment from God to spot wolves in sheep's clothing. God has equipped every healthy pastor with the ability to see these people who may have hidden agendas and impure motives. Always trust your pastor's guidance.

4. Lead songs the congregation knows. Obviously, the leading of the Holy Spirit takes precedence over all of this. I never want to get so strict with these rules that it puts the Holy Spirit in a position where He can't come in and do whatever He wants. As a general rule of thumb, a new song needs be taught to the Church at least every other week. I rarely will do more than two brand new songs at any event. The Bride needs to be able to sing to her Bridegroom, and if she does not know the songs, she probably will not sing. On this note it is also very important that you pay attention to the type of audience that you are leading in worship. For instance, if you are leading in front of an elderly crowd, lead songs that they would know, like "The Old Rugged Cross." You can't expect too much engagement from an older demographic if you are leading a more contemporary song like "Oceans (Where Feet May Fail)" from Hillsong. Also, make sure the words are being displayed properly somewhere in the building. Again, the Bride needs to sing to her Bridegroom and if she does not know the lyrics she probably will not sing. If the Holy Spirit moves in a powerful way, and the time comes for a spontaneous song that has never been sung before, then again, all of this gets thrown out of the window.

5. People in your band with a good ear for sound need to step away from their instruments and get on the audience-side of the speakers and listen to the mix at least once a month. Does it sound good or bad? Are there any instruments dominating the others? Is the mix overall too loud or too soft for the size building you are in? If you do not have a sound engineer on staff at your church I recommend hiring one to come in at least once or twice a year to conduct routine sound checks. Think of this the way you think of getting an oil change for your car. It never hurts to have things inspected by a professional.

6. Make sure you put markings or some form of identification to differentiate between music gear that belongs to volunteering individuals and music gear that belongs to the church. This will save you a lot of trouble. Churches, it may be a good idea to take inventory of all you have so that you can make sure nothing is being taken. Many times music gear is left at a church building by a volunteer musician who paid for the gear with their own money. Soon after, their gear is thrown in with the gear the church owns. Try to avoid these mix-ups as best as you can.

8. Sound technicians: Pay attention and stay engaged during the service. Constantly be scanning the platform. Sitting in the back behind the sound board is not an excuse to drift off, text or play games on your phone. Nothing is more embarrassing for you and your pastor when he or she walks up to the microphone and it is not on because you weren't paying attention. If you feel overwhelmed behind the soundboard, then start training others who can help you. Don't become possessive over your own territory, or else it will soon possess you.

9. Always be looking for ways to grow your team. Worship leaders, you cannot feel threatened by those that God has placed beneath you to train up and nurture. You must always be seeking out ways you can effectively grow and expand your team. Be thinking of the future. What can you do to make the church you are serving as solid as possible, just in case you miss a Sunday, or one day transition to another assignment God has for you?

FOOD FOR THOUGHT
QUESTION & ANSWER TIME

1. How punctual is your worship team?

2. Is there a waiting period for musicians and/or singers who want to join your worship team?

3. Have musicians and/or singers interested in joining your worship team demonstrated a commitment to your church?

4. Sound technicians and lyric operators, do you give your full attention during every service?

19

The Sound That Jesus Died to Hear Is the Sound of His Bride

In order to defend the purity of worship properly, we need to always remember who worship belongs to. It all belongs to Jesus. Secondly, we need to remember exactly what it is that Jesus longs to hear when He is worshipped. Jesus did not die for a piano, nor did He die for a guitar. Jesus did not die for a platform, nor did He die for a microphone. Jesus did not die for an amazing sound system, nor did He die for a drum set. Jesus did not die for a bass, nor did He die for an organ.

Of all the amazing sounds a worship team can produce on a Sunday morning, none is more pleasing to His ears than the voice of His bride, the Church of Jesus Christ singing His praises. He paid with his own lifeblood to hear this sound.

Just think about it. Until Jesus died, there never was a Church that He could hear singing to Him.

The Church is made up of those who were once bound in chains, but now are able to dance before Him in freedom. She was once silenced in fear and oppression, but now she is able to sing to Him, liberated with a heart full of joy. She was once captive to her sin, but now she is able to sing to Him a song of redemption and deliverance.

Worship leaders never ever forget this. The enemy will always come and tempt you to make worship all about you, or all about the performance, or all about the instruments, or all about everything else besides her singing to Him, His Bride. We cannot forget, at the end of the day, the sound of His Bride singing is more beautiful to Him than the best guitar solo. It is more beautiful to Him than the most heavenly sounding piano. It is more beautiful to Him than the best solo singing performance. **The Bride of Christ lifting her voice as one is the sound that He paid with His own lifeblood to hear.**

FOOD FOR THOUGHT
QUESTION & ANSWER TIME

1. Church sound systems today can be loud. How often do you bring down the volume level of the band during a worship set so the audience can participate and be heard?

2. As a worship leader, does it excite you as much to have the church audience involved with the worship set as it would if an amazing musician had joined your team for a set?

20

Real Worship Looks Like the Pure Life Jesus Lived

Worshippers, the one common thing that God the Father desires to see in all of us who are in worship ministries is Jesus. Jesus is the perfect example of what worship really looks like. He is the ultimate defender of the purity of worship, and He earned this right by never doing one thing for Himself while He was here on the Earth. Jesus did every little thing for the glory of His Father. To live a life like this is the greatest act of worship. This is becoming a living sacrifice.

What God wants to know today is what measure of Jesus are we carrying? To what degree has His nature taken over ours? Without a doubt, I know the more our flesh dies, the more His Spirit can take over. If the nature of Jesus is not being played out in our day-to-day life, then our worship on

Sunday mornings is not pure at all.

It may seem like a daunting task to live a life that brings God glory in all things as Jesus did. I can promise you that this task is always most daunting to those who do not want to surrender and die to their flesh. If you are okay with dying to your flesh and submitting to the leading of the Holy Spirit, then you will have no problem becoming a living sacrifice. We as worship leaders and psalmists were not called to change *somewhat* in our natures, or die to our flesh *little by little*. From the very beginning of our new birth in Christ we were called to completely die to our flesh. This is exactly why we all had to be born again. Just think about it. It makes no sense for someone to be reborn unless they have first died. What is the death someone dies before being born again? The death of their flesh.

This kind of extreme surrender does not equate to having a boring robotic life. In fact, it is quite the opposite. When we live for God like this, our lives will be filled with more peace and joy than ever! When we have experienced the new birth of God's Spirit and have allowed the nature of Christ to take over ours, then our worship on Sunday mornings will be the best it's ever been. Why? Because, when we get up to minister to the Lord, we will have the confident assurance that our daily lives are truly pleasing to Him.

On the opposite end of the spectrum, when there is sin

in our lives, and we are aware of it by the Holy Spirit, there is little or no enjoyment in our worship. Instead, there is only the burden of conviction and an overwhelming sense to get the problem taken care of. No wonder Jesus commanded us to leave our offerings at the altar and make things right if we know we have sin in our lives. God wants us to truly enjoy worshipping Him and being in His presence.

If someone teaches you that it is okay for you to bring your offering to God, when you know you have unaddressed sin in your life, that person lacks understanding of the Word of God. No amount of worshipping God or bringing Him sacrifices can ever cover your sin. *"Does the LORD delight in burnt offerings and sacrifices as much as in obeying the LORD? To obey is better than sacrifice, and to heed is better than the fat of rams."* (1 Samuel 15:22 NIV) *"Who may ascend the mountain of the Lord? Who may stand in his holy place? The one who has clean hands and a pure heart, who does not trust in an idol or swear by a false god. They will receive blessing from the Lord and vindication from God their Savior."* (Psalm 24:3-5 NIV) Jesus clearly taught on purity and how purity is the one way we get to see God: *"Blessed are the pure in heart, for they will see God."* (Matthew 5:8 NIV) God wants your first act of worship to Him to be that your heart is pure and your life is blameless. Only then are we allowed to ascend the Holy mountain of God and partake in the deep things of the Spirit.

FOOD FOR THOUGHT
QUESTION & ANSWER TIME

1. Do you live a life of obedience unto the Lord? How much of your nature has been overtaken by the nature of Christ?

2. Is there any part of your life that you know needs to die to sin?

3. Is your life blameless? When's the last time you went through everything in your life and did a checkup to make sure it was clean?

21

Newsflash! People Get Saved When We Worship!

This chapter is so important for every worship leader to read. I cannot stress this enough. When you are called to lead worship, it is an easy thing to believe that you are not a great harvester of souls. In light of this, I want to start this section off with a very real scenario I often faced as a worship leader. It all began with the thought I used to have that my work in worship was not as important, or as effective, as the work of a pastor or an evangelist.

When you have thoughts like this, that raise questions as to whether or not what you're doing is of any Kingdom value, you have fallen into a not-so-good place. Fortunately, it is an easy fix to get out of that place.

As a worship leader, or a musician, sometimes thoughts can

creep into your mind like: "You are not really doing anything for the Kingdom. You aren't out there on the mission field." Or, "You're not the evangelist who is presenting the Gospel right now. What good is your worship?" These attacks against the mind of the worship leader can lead to self-mutilating thoughts that are extremely unhealthy and may even lead to carelessness or backsliding. As I just said, the good news is that the Truth of the Word of God can easily dispel this darkness.

I would like to show you a scripture concerning the New Covenant, which we live under now, and the plans God has for worship. This scripture is taken from Acts, chapter 15:12-18 NIV, when the early Church was having a discussion and James spoke up to quote a prophecy from the book of Amos.

The whole assembly became silent as they listened to Barnabas and Paul telling about the signs and wonders God had done among the Gentiles through them. When they finished, James spoke up. "Brothers," he said, "listen to me. Simon has described to us how God first intervened to choose a people for his name from the Gentiles. The words of the prophets are in agreement with this, as it is written: "'After this I will return and rebuild David's fallen tent. Its ruins I will rebuild, and I will restore it, that the rest of mankind may seek the Lord, even all the Gentiles who bear my name, says the Lord, who does these things' - things known from long ago."

You see, no wonder the Devil spends so much time attacking and discouraging those who are like David, generation after generation. He knows that the restoration of the tabernacle of David will bring about a mighty harvest for the Lord's glory. Pastors! If you want to see many souls saved in your church, pour into your worship team and make sure their fires are burning red hot. **Real worship always invites the Presence of God, and wherever the Presence of God is there is guaranteed victory.** If we want to win this world for Jesus, we need the Presence of God with us. Without His Presence, no song, no message and no man carries any life-changing power. It is His presence, Him just being there, that brings the victory. So, if we want more of His presence, let us bring to Him more of our praises, more of our worship and more of ourselves as a living sacrifice.

There is also a warning that is hidden within the prophecy of Amos concerning the Tabernacle of David: If people get saved when music that glorifies the Lord is playing, what do you think happens when music that glorifies something else is playing? We ought to always remember that everything glorifies something. If something does not bring glory to God, we must quickly find out what it's bringing glory to.

QUESTION & ANSWER TIME

1. As a worshipper, do you sometimes struggle with feelings that you are not doing much for the Kingdom?

2. Are you aware of the many different things David did and presented before God as his worship? Look at the book of 1 Chronicles, beginning in chapter 13, to see the creativity of David's worship.

3. How would this kind of 24/7 worship apply to your life today?

22

All a Church Needs to Inspire Them to Worship Is to See Jesus

If you were to put **King David** in a mod-ern day **American church I guarantee you that most Pastors would be embarrassed by his worship and ashamed to have him as a member of the congregation.** David would not even care because his heart would be so captured by the beauty of God.

When you are worshipping God in purity, it becomes very hard to remember who is watching you. King David was so punch drunk on God's love that he did things for God in public that no one had ever done before. In 2 Samuel chapter 6 it is recorded that David danced so wildly before God that his clothes fell off. What inspires the kind of worship David offered to God? What makes a person sing a song with all of their might and a heart full of thanksgiving? What makes them jump up and down and spin around wildly in exuberant joy?

Worship like David's is inspired by holiness so magnificent that all one can do is bow down and break open. Worship like David's is triggered by beauty so stunning that no man can describe it in any language. Worship like David's is ignited by love so perfect, and kindness so unimaginable, that it makes the greatest love shown by any person on earth seem microscopic. There are not enough earthly or Heavenly languages to ascribe to Jesus the beauty of His holiness. So again, why did David do all that He did when he worshipped? Simply because of Jesus.

Let's shift gears here and think about something for a moment. Imagine what you are going to see when your eyes first look upon Jesus. Just think about that. When you see Him in all the fullness of His beauty and majesty, what's it going to look like? Imagine a thousand sunrises all at once, and then multiply that by a million more. His beauty will be like nothing your eyes have ever seen before. It will be so stunning that your heart is literally going to feel like exploding, as you try your best to look upon His radiant face.

When you behold Him imagine what you are going to feel. You are literally going to feel His being, the love of all loves, emanating from Him, the source of it all. When you see Him, not only are you going to see Him, but you are going to quite literally **feel** Him. What you're going to feel is going to shock you. His love for you will be so intense that your soul will feel like fainting. Your heart will be quaking, and even in your Heavenly body, you will have a shortness of breath, as you feel in its fullness, what you have always longed to feel, an absolutely perfect love, right there in person. This alone is what inspired the kind of worship David gave. We worship not because we were trained, taught or forced. We worship because He is far lovelier than the loveliest thing this universe has to offer.

Worship is just what we do in response to all that He is. The angels who are forever singing "Holy, holy, holy" are just as alive as you and I are right now. They are not robotic, lifeless, pre-programmed beings. They have real senses like you and I and real decision-making capabilities like you and I. The elders who are continually before the throne bowing down day and night are not doing what they're doing because someone told them to. When you stand before such an awesome God, and all of your senses (your sight, hearing, taste, touch and smell) are constantly bombarded by His glory, all you can do is one thing – worship! **When you see Him, all that is left to do is worship!**

A good friend of mine once told me: **"So many think that the pinnacle or the peak of worship is that we get to see God. We don't worship so that we can see God, we worship because we have seen God, and what we have seen is**

so beautiful and so amazing that all we can do is worship Him." - Stone Meyer

Therefore, the mandate of every worship leader, musician and singer in the church is to understand who God is and how great He is. Then, gently turn the face of the Church to the position of being perfectly fixed on Him. May the worship leader who seeks to turn the face of the Church to his or herself be awakened by the Holy Spirit to the horrible sin they are committing. We do not lead worship to turn the face of the Church towards ourselves, but unto Him.

FOOD FOR THOUGHT
QUESTION & ANSWER TIME

1. How much of your worship set on Sundays is centered on ascribing glory and honor to Jesus? When is the last time you gave your church a good description of who He is?

2. How much time do you spend seeking God and being in His presence alone, outside of the organized worship set?

3. In leading worship, how difficult will it be for you to present a proper picture of who Jesus is to the church if you are not spending time alone with God?

23

Let's Worship God in Spirit and in
Truth - Not in Soul and in Truth

This chapter was written out of a conversation I had with a friend of mine from Argentina, Gustavo Braun. I was telling Pastor
Gustavo how in the late Spring of 2015 I ran
into a major problem as a worship leader.

As a leader I naturally want to get to as many new songs
as possible to keep things fresh. The kind of songs I look for
and love are the ones that are all about Jesus, the ones that are
totally centered on Him. I told Gustavo how in today's world
and especially on Christian radio there really aren't that many
of these songs being heard. I told him how hard it was for me
to find songs that are all about God's holiness and His beauty.

To be honest, I was getting a little upset as I was talking to
him. I continued, telling him how I have no problem finding
plenty of Christian songs that are all about me and my issues,

the kind of songs that are all about what I am going through and how God fits into my world, not how I fit into His goodness.

Gustavo's response to my observation was absolutely incredible. In broken English he said something like this: "Phil, I want you to think of the words in most worship songs you hear nowadays. Do you ever listen to one worship song and it is really, really anointed and then you go to listen to another and it is not quite there? Why is that?" I paused and thought about it for a moment and he went on: "Many people like to sing about how **they** are touched emotionally in worship and many people like to sing about what they think about God, even though what they think falls short of the Word. Instead of keeping the attention on Jesus, they somehow find a way to continually write songs that are actually about themselves." As he was speaking, he was putting into words what I had felt for so long, but never was able to articulate: "Many people sing songs that are almost about God, but aren't, and I don't even think they realize it. They're singing about a river, about an atmosphere, or about what's going on in the world. It's as if the song almost got there, but it didn't quite take off. The song never got off of the ground and onto His beauty."

Gustavo went on to deliver the final punch line, which is the reason for this chapter: "Phil, here is the main reason why these kinds of songs fall short, the main reason why you and so many others who deeply love God do not like them: Our thoughts, our emotions and our feelings, all of these things, do not come from the Spirit. These are all things that come from the soul." Gustavo then quoted a scripture: *"Jesus said: 'Yet a time is coming and has now come when the true worshipers will worship the Father in the Spirit and in truth, for they are the kind of worshipers the Fathers seeks.'"* (John 4:23 NIV)

Gustavo continued, "Phil, God our Father does not like worship from the place of the soul as much as He does from the deepest place, the spirit."

This is the one revelation that the Christian music industry needs to hear so badly: The Father seeks worship in Spirit and in Truth, not in soul and in Truth. To truly worship someone who lives in the spirit, your worship must come from the Spirit and not from the soul, which is your thoughts, your emotions and your feelings. Can your soul be involved? Absolutely. David said things like this over and over again: *"And my soul shall be joyful in the LORD: it shall rejoice in his salvation."* (Psalm 35:9 NIV) Having the soul involved and engaged in worship is never a bad thing. Just make sure your spirit and the Truth of God's Word are leading the charge, and not your soul.

Why then, when you flip on the radio, are there so many hit Christian artists singing soul-led songs and not spirit-led songs?

Why in the world are songs like this so popular? Soul-led song-writers are more of a hit than Spirit-led songwriters, because in America the soul-led Church is much larger than the Spirit-led Church. Does that mean that the soul-led church is not saved? No, not at all, but it does mean that a significant part of our body is in great need of awakening when it comes to worship. Worship leaders, let's make it our mission to be extra careful and extra picky when we are choosing songs to lead on Sundays. Let's make sure they are songs that please the Spirit of God and proclaim God's Truth not songs that glorify the temporal sufferings of this life.

FOOD FOR THOUGHT
QUESTION & ANSWER TIME

1. What kind of screening process do you have in place to determine what songs you will lead at your church?

2. Are there any songs you play at church that, upon second glance, you realize are not even about Jesus at all?

24

But *Why* Does God Seek Worship in Spirit and in Truth?

"*Yet a time is coming and has now come when the true worshipers will worship the Father in the Spirit and in truth, for they are the kind of worshipers the Father seeks.*" (John 4:23 NIV) I heard this verse so much growing up and always wondered what it really meant. Why does our Father seek worshippers who will worship Him in Spirit and in Truth? Then, one day while reading this verse, the Lord opened my eyes.

The reason our Father seeks those who will worship Him in Spirit and in Truth is because Spirit and Truth are the other two parts of the Trinity that He has released upon the earth. In keeping His word as Emmanuel, God with us, the Father has sent His precious Son, Jesus, and His Holy Spirit to us. Therefore, what real worship looks like to the Father is a life that is completely taken over and hidden in the Spirit and the Son. What God wants to see in us as worshippers is evidence of what He has sent of Himself to earth.

When Jesus was speaking of worship in Spirit, He was obviously referring to the Holy Spirit. When Jesus was speaking of worship in Truth, He was speaking of the Word of God, or Himself. The Greek word used when Jesus said "Spirit" is the word *pneuma* which means "a blast of breath from God, Christ's Spirit, or the Holy Spirit." When Jesus said "Truth," it was the Greek word *altheia,* which is the same word Jesus used when He said "I am the Truth." (I am the Altheia) When Jesus said "Spirit and Truth" He wasn't merely talking about things you **do** when you worship, he was quite literally talking about people, Himself and the Holy Spirit. When the Father is looking into your worship, what He is seeking to see is "Spirit and Truth."

This really changes things up when we realize what Jesus was talking about in John 4:23. No longer is our worship just about music, but it is now centered on our very communion with God the Father, Himself. The Bible says that there is nothing good in man. So, when we worship in Spirit and in Truth, it is evidence that the two persons of the Trinity our Father sent to earth are at work in us. Spirit and Truth literally make up for what we are missing when we worship. When we worship in Spirit and in Truth it also shows the world that we really belong to our Father and not to this world. The Father is inseparable from His Son and from His Spirit, so when we worship in Spirit and in Truth it means that we have become inseparable from Him.

What's so amazing is that our Father, to this very day, is still seeking out people to invite into this fellowship with Him. He is looking for those who want to experience the fullness of who He is by the Son and the Holy Spirit. Those who walk in this fellowship are His true offspring, His real children. Popular teaching in the world today says that we are all children of God but this is not true. The scriptures say: *"Yet to all who did receive him, to those who believed in his name, he gave the right to become children of God."* (John 1:12 NIV)

So how does worship in Spirit and Truth play into a Sunday morning set? First, we need to have deep communion with the Holy Spirit, so that we may know His voice and His leading. You can't follow someone's voice you aren't familiar with hearing. In the same way, you cannot have Spirit-led worship without first being a Spirit-follower. The easiest way to lead a church congregation in worship is by following the Spirit.

Secondly, we need the Truth, or the Word of God, in our songs and our sermons. The Word of God is anointed all by itself. **Anyone** can read the Word of God out loud, and chains will break. When we choose to sing songs with the Word of God as the lyrical content, we are literally singing Jesus, since He is the Word made flesh. These are the two most practical ways that Spirit and Truth can play into our music.

More importantly than the music, before you even lift your voice in song, are you letting Spirit and Truth, the Holy Spirit and the Son, have command over your life? **Surely, if our worship is not in Spirit and in Truth, it is not the kind of worship the Father is seeking. If we don't worship in Spirit and in Truth, then we are not the kind of worshippers the Father is seeking.**

There is no getting around the words Jesus spoke when he described the kind of worshippers the Father is looking for. The kind of worship leader the world wants has always been very different from the kind of worship leader the Father wants. *"But the Lord said to Samuel, 'Do not look at his appearance or at his physical stature, because I have refused him. For the Lord does not see as man sees; for man looks at the outward appearance, but the Lord looks at the heart.'"* (1 Samuel 16:7 NKJV) The world wants the next supermodel that can play a guitar solo like Jimmy Paige and sing like Steve Perry, but the Father? Frankly, He is not impressed by any of these gifts, because He's the one that gave them in the first place. What really impresses God is a heart that's totally His and a heart that will obey Him.

FOOD FOR THOUGHT

QUESTION & ANSWER TIME

1. Have you truly surrendered to the Holy Spirit and the Son? As you look over your life, do you know in your heart that you have obeyed Him completely?

2. Why do you worship? What drives you to play music on Sundays?

3. Do you view everything that you do as an opportunity to bring God glory? Do you see everything you do as an opportunity to worship Him and have fellowship by His Spirit and His Truth?

25

We Must Honor the Gifts
of God In One Another

If we are to defend the purity of worship, we must defend each other. The world says to climb the ladder of success, even at the expense of those closest to you. In God's Kingdom, there is no such strife, because there is plenty of room for everyone.

Within His Kingdom He alone assigns the work to each of His children, and from the greatest to the least, everyone who is part of His Kingdom is a servant, one to another. When you see a minister, or a ministry, that has become successful at the expense of others in the Kingdom, tread carefully around them, because that method should be foreign to the Kingdom of God.

The most important aspect of our worship is obviously found in what is going on between us and God. For example, we know when we come before God we have to have clean hands and a pure heart. A second, and equally important part of our worship is what is going on between ourselves and others. If our relationships on earth stink, and we treat people like garbage, what makes us think that God is going to be excited to receive our praises? A wise pastor from Argentina named Pedro Ibarra once told me: **"The anointing does not carry character but character carries the anointing."**

Worshippers, what I would like to talk about in this chapter is honoring each other and how important this is if we are to function as a healthy unit. The Kingdom of God functions best when we are all working together and not against each other. When we honor each other in the Body of Christ we honor Christ Himself. I must, when I look at anyone in His body, realize that the same price Jesus paid for my soul He also paid for theirs. This price He paid for each of us, who are His, cannot be measured by any measure of worldly currency. So, when we show honor to each other, we are showing honor to the price He paid.

Some of you know very well the gifts of God inside of you, while some of you are still figuring that out. We must always be looking to call out the golden gifts that God has placed within our brothers and sisters. The easiest way for a leader to pull the gifts of God out from within someone else is to honor them. Leaders, if you have a team that is struggling to produce fruit, ask yourself: **"When was the last time I honored my team members, honored the gifts of God inside of them, and honored the price God paid for them? When was the last time I set aside a portion of our practice to openly speak blessings over them and build them up?"**

Some of you worship leaders and musicians may have never had a man of God look at you in the eye and ask you: "Do you know who you really are? Do you realize the greatness of the gift of God that lies upon you?" You may have never experienced someone honoring you in such a way. Let me tell you some really Good News. Jesus Christ, the King of Kings and Lord of Lords, has already honored you. He has honored you with His own lifeblood. The value of all that you are is found in the price that Jesus has paid for you. The price He paid for you was everything.

FOOD FOR THOUGHT
QUESTION & ANSWER TIME

1. Do you take time to honor those around you?

2. Do you see others through the eyes of the blood of Jesus? Do you see others as being worth His life?

26

The Modern-Day Basics of Running and Operating a Worship Team - Part 3

This is the last section where I will provide practical instruction on how to successfully run a worship team. I cannot stress enough the importance of establishing good habits. The small healthy habits you establish will lead to great Kingdom success.

Let's take a look at these last few points on how to run a healthy worship team:

1. Put into writing the standards of your church's worship ministry. Write out everything that is expected. Make everything clear to each person who is interested in joining. I would even have your new worship team members and current worship team members sign a copy of these standards, stating that they have read what is expected of them and that they agree. Always keep these signed copies on file. It is always good to cover your back and have a plan to defend yourself in the event of an uprising.

2. People on the platform, please dress to represent Jesus. I love to wear tank tops in the summer, but I will personally not wear them while leading worship. Women, please cover up. I am not saying you all need to wear a suit, just remember that you are there to bring attention to Jesus, not to yourself.

3. Take a break and do something fun as a team every now and then. Get to know one another. Once every couple of months, instead of having a practice, have a team get together and go out to eat. Go do something fun to strengthen friendships and community. Also, schedule times where you can have your lead pastor come in and address your team. Always make room for him to share his heart and minister to you all. As worship teams, you all pour out a lot, so take some time to drink in.

4. Paid worship ministers and musicians: Do not think like an employee. Even though you're being paid, choose to think like a minister. This point was a great revelation shared with me by my friend Sergio Scataglini. An employee makes sure that what THEY have to do gets done. A minister sees the bigger picture and has no problem being flexible for the

Kingdom. Imagine this scenario with me: A pastor asks a worship leader to do something for the church at a time when he or she is supposed to be doing something else, like a worship practice. An employee minded worship leader will become defensive and territorial towards the pastor saying: "But hey, we have practice that night, we can't go and do what you want us to do." If that worship leader instead started thinking like a minister, they would see the bigger picture of the Kingdom and would no longer be territorial and defensive.

5. Worship team members: Serve in other areas of the church. Personally, I will not let anyone be a part of my team if they are not willing to serve in other areas of the church. Christ the King is the servant of all, so we must serve also. This can look like serving as an usher, volunteering for church projects, or serving in a food pantry.

6. Practice and refine your musical skills on your own time. Do not use rehearsal time to learn how to play your instrument. There is nothing that slows down a practice more than trying to figure out parts that you should have figured out on your own time. Practice time should be used for bringing everything together and finalizing song material, not for last minute cramming.

7. Be honest with yourselves, and be real with your life schedule. Do not sacrifice your higher priorities so you can be on the worship team. If you do not have the time to get better at your instrument or show up to practice because you have work or family commitments, do not sweat it. These things need your attention first. Be faithful with what God has already given you before trying to add more to your plate.

8. Clean out your social media. I cannot stress the importance of this enough. Go through all of your past posts and clean house. Again, everyone is watching you and following your example so please be careful what you put on social media. If you have to ask yourself "Is this something I should post or not?" then it probably is not.

9. Don't be afraid to write songs and try them out. Make sure they are in line with the Word of God and go for it. Pay attention as you "test-drive" them and be open to critique and feedback. If your congregation catches on to something quick and starts singing along, then run with it and develop the idea.

FOOD FOR THOUGHT

QUESTION & ANSWER TIME

1. Do you put in writing the kind of behavior expected of your worship team?

2. When was the last time your entire worship team got together to fellowship and hang out?

3. Is there anyone on your worship team overwhelmed by outside commitments, which often interferes with their commitments to the worship team? Remember that dedication to families and faithfulness to work must come first. If we don't honor the people God's put in our lives, then we are not honoring God at all.

4. When was the last time your worship team tried to play an original song written from within your church?

27

come

Before Anything Else
You Are His Child

If we are to defend the purity of worship properly, we must have our identity in line with the Word of God. Jesus was not God the Father's "Appointed Rabbi" (although that was a function of Jesus). Jesus was not God the Father's "Anointed Prophet" (although that was also a function of Jesus). Jesus was not God the Father's "Glorious Evangelist" (although that was also a function of Jesus). God the Father made it clear on more than one occasion that Jesus was His "Beloved Son."

Why didn't God proclaim from Heaven: "This is my Appointed Teacher, hear Him?" Or why didn't He say: "This is my Wonderful Minister of the Gospel in whom I am well pleased?" If God had done that, it would have been silly and shallow. We all know there is no way God would have spoken that over Jesus. **So, why do so many of us place more pride and emphasis on being called a worship leader, a prophet or an apostle than being called a son or a daughter?** If Jesus is your Lord, then you are an adopted child of God the Father, and just as He did with Jesus, God the Father wants to call you His son or His daughter before He calls you anything else.

Here's why: You may be a very prophetic person, but don't cling too tightly to that gift, because one day when you go home to Heaven you won't be needing it anymore. You may be a person who is very gifted in healing and miracles, but don't let your identity get wrapped too tightly in that, because one day when you go home to Heaven you won't be needing it anymore. Although the gifts of the Spirit are wonderful, and much needed in the world today, it alarms me how so many who walk in their gifts are okay with not living holy lives. I am baffled at how so many who are so spiritually gifted have no integrity and show no honor to their brothers and sisters. The root of this problem is that someone who has a strong spiritual gift has latched their pride and identity onto that gift, instead of latching it onto the revelation of being a son or a daughter of God.

The world may try to label you as a worship leader, a music

director, a singer, a pastor, an evangelist, but that is the lesser title. The greater title was revealed to you by God Himself, and that Heavenly title is that **YOU** are His beloved child. All of Hell toils, day and night, to plant seeds of doubt and unbelief in your heart against this. The truth of who we are is what really sets us free. In case you need a reminder, here is just a little bit of the truth about who you really are:

You are a Child of God, therefore when you worship, His presence fills the room.

You are a Child of God, therefore when you cry out and lift your voice to Him, your Heavenly Father responds.

You are a Child of God, therefore when you stand firm and oppose a stronghold, it will be torn down.

You are a Child of God, therefore where you go, His Kingdom goes.

Before you are anything else, **YOU** are His beloved child.

FOOD FOR THOUGHT
QUESTION & ANSWER TIME

1. Do you really believe that you are a child of God?

2. What means more to you; being a Child of God, or having some other well-known ministry title?

3. If your heart is not moved by the awesomeness of being God's child, what can you do to change your priorities?

28

The Potential in Your
Heart to Move God

More than your musical style or your ability to play an instrument, your heart possesses the ability to move God. **God is not moved by the music someone is playing unless the heart of that person behind the music is moved by Him.** If someone is hungry, they are going to find food or go to their kitchen and cook something. The same is true for worship. No one really worships until they are hungry to do so. Any real act of worship begins in the unseen depths of someone's heart long before it makes its way out into the visible world.

When we approach worship this way, it doesn't really matter how talented or gifted we are. Therefore, those who feel like they need to be doing something on the platform all the time are usually desiring so for the wrong reason. Remember what Jesus said: *"When you are invited to a wedding feast, don't sit in the seat of honor. What if someone who is more distinguished than you has also been invited? The host will come and say, 'Give this person your seat.' Then you will be embarrassed, and you will have to take whatever seat is left at the foot of the table! "Instead, take the lowest place at the foot of the table. Then when your host sees you, he will come and say, 'Friend, we have a better place for you!' Then you will be honored in front of all the other guests. For those who exalt themselves will be humbled, and those who humble themselves will be exalted."* (Luke 14:8-11 NLT) If Jesus tells us to desire the lowest place at a wedding dinner, then shouldn't we be doing the same with our church platforms?

Far too many worship leaders have taken the highest place on the platform and fallen in love with it. A worship leader who refuses to serve others is too wrapped in his or her gifting, and if they do not change they will one day be humbled by God. I know for a fact that I have strong musical gifts and talents, but I've realized that these things aren't really all that important. I know if I woke up tomorrow, and somehow I was a tree, I would still praise God with my whole wooden heart. I do not know what all I could do to praise God as a tree, but I would stay rooted in his love, and in my woody heart I would still be shouting: "I love You Father with my whole heart!'"

When David said: "Bless the Lord oh my soul!" He was talking about something genuine that was happening on the inside of him in the unseen place of his soul. What is happening on the inside of you that is unseen by others? Is your soul blessing God? Are your thoughts thinking of God? Only you can hold yourself accountable here. It is a shame that some people get up to lead worship, singing everything right and saying everything right, but inwardly have no heart for God.

An absent heart that is far from the Lord, or disengaged in worship, does not have any place in a worship setting. I would rather hear a 100-year-old lady lead, singing a worship song with tears flowing down her face, lost in love with Jesus, than the biggest and most popular band singing their hit song if they have no passion at all for Jesus. I would rather hear a broken hallelujah from the lips of a soon-to-be martyr, who has nothing left but a heart that loves Jesus, than the most influential worship group singing without a hint of what it means to bring a real sacrifice to Jesus. So often in the Body of Christ we get so caught up in the programs, the set list, the sounds and the structure, and those are all good things that I enjoy having, but we cannot forget about our hearts. **We were not saved to sing songs - we were saved to be totally in love with our Father.**

Have you ever pondered the fact that Jesus never once talked about music and worship together? Think about that for a minute. Jesus never once talked about worship being primarily musical. Some of the best Biblical references for music-based worship can be found in scripture related to the life of King David. But let me ask you this: **What do you think it was that God really loved about King David, His heart or his musical ability? Did God love David's passion for Him, or the fact that David could play the harp well and write songs?**

If we were really honest, we would all agree that what God really loved about David, was not his ability to play music, but his heart for His Presence. I guarantee you, if David's gifting was painting beautiful pictures for the Lord, we would all want to be painting in our worship services today. If you have a heart like David, you can do just about **anything** for the Lord and it will be pleasing to Him.

Before you sing with your voice on Sundays, double check to see if your heart is singing a song to Him first. Before you play your instrument on Sundays, double check to see if your heart is playing a tune for Him first. Let what comes out of your hands and feet and mouth be from a heart that truly does want to bless the Lord! When we do this, God's response to our worship will be phenomenal.

FOOD FOR THOUGHT
QUESTION & ANSWER TIME

1. Before you worship God, do you look at your heart long and hard enough to make sure that your primary focus is loving God with all that you are?

29

Holding up the Standard of the Levites - Part 1

When defending the purity of worship, there are certain adjustments God will ask us to make that may be difficult. These adjustments date all the way back to the beginning of corporate worship. The first written recordings of corporate worship can be found when the children of Israel left Egypt and entered the desert.

When the Israelites left Egypt, there was no prescribed way to minister to the Lord. All of mankind was completely clueless as to how to be in God's presence, and they were even more clueless as to what God expected once they were there.

The Levites were the first group of people, since the fall of man, collectively allowed the privilege of being in the Presence of God. It is written of the Levites: *"At that time the Lord set apart the tribe of Levi to carry the ark of the covenant of the Lord, to stand before the Lord to serve Him and to bless in His name until this day. Therefore, Levites do not have a portion or inheritance with their brothers; the Lord is their inheritance, just as the Lord your God spoke to him."* (Deuteronomy 10:8-9 NIV) And it is also written: *"Only the Levites shall perform the service of the tent of meeting (the place where God's presence dwelt), and they shall bear the iniquity of the people; it shall be a perpetual statute throughout your generations, and among the sons of Israel they shall have no inheritance. For the tithe of the sons of Israel, which they offer as an offering to the Lord, I have given to the Levites for an inheritance; therefore I have said concerning them, they shall have no inheritance among the sons of Israel."* (For the Lord is their inheritance) (Numbers 18:23-24 NIV)

Why is this? Why did the Levites get the Lord Himself as their inheritance when no one else in Israel did? Why did they get to worship in God's presence when no one else was allowed to? Why did God love them so much that He would say: *"The tithe that men bring to me, the Levites can have all of it."* For God to want to give you all of the money that was originally set aside for Him you must have done something to seriously touch His heart. Let's take a look at the incredible story from Exodus 32:1-29 NIV, which shows us exactly how the Levites earned their set apart place with God:

When the people saw that Moses was so long in coming down from the mountain, they gathered around Aaron and said, "Come, make us a god who will go before us. As for this fellow Moses who brought us up out of Egypt, we don't know what has happened to him." Aaron answered them, "Take off the gold earrings that your wives, your sons and your daughters are wearing, and bring them to me." So all the people took off their earrings and brought them to Aaron. He took what they handed him and made it into an idol cast in the shape of a calf, fashioning it with a tool. Then they said, "These are your gods, Israel, who brought you up out of Egypt." When Aaron saw this, he built an altar in front of the calf and announced, "Tomorrow there will be a festival to the Lord." So the next day the people rose early and sacrificed burnt offerings and presented fellowship offerings. Afterward they sat down to eat and drink and got up to indulge in revelry. Then the Lord said to Moses, "Go down, because your people, whom you brought up out of Egypt, have become corrupt. They have been quick to turn away from what I commanded them and have made themselves an idol cast in the shape of a calf. They have bowed down to it and sacrificed to it and have said, 'These are your gods, Israel, who brought you up out of Egypt.'"

(Skipping down a few verses - Moses comes down the mountain, furious with Israel)

"Do not be angry, my lord," Aaron answered. "You know how prone these people are to evil. They said to me, 'Make us gods who will go before us. As for this fellow Moses who brought us up out of Egypt, we don't know what has happened to him.' So I told them, 'Whoever has

any gold jewelry, take it off.' Then they gave me the gold, and I threw it into the fire, and out came this calf!"

Moses saw that the people were running wild and that Aaron had let them get out of control and so become a laughingstock to their enemies. So he stood at the entrance to the camp and said, "Whoever is for the Lord, come to me." And all the Levites rallied to him. Then he said to them (the Levites), "This is what the Lord, the God of Israel, says: 'Each man strap a sword to his side. Go back and forth through the camp from one end to the other, each killing his brother and friend and neighbor.'" The Levites did as Moses commanded, and that day about three thousand of the people died. Then Moses said, "You have been set apart to the Lord today, for you were against your own sons and brothers, and he has blessed you this day."

This image of the Levites turning on their own brothers and sisters for the sake of righteousness is so powerful. The Levites were not afraid to defend the purity of worship. I cannot stress enough the importance of their willingness to do this. I am not suggesting that we all strap swords to our sides and slay all of our ungodly relatives. That's the last thing I want us to do. The imagery provided here is what needs to happen in our minds and our hearts when we decide to follow Jesus.

Anything that stands against Jesus, that may hold us back from Him, needs to be removed from our lives. Why? Because sin is rebellion, and to disobey God is to request that His very presence be dismissed from our midst. In fact, to the dismay of the Israelites, that is exactly what God did shortly after this incident: (God speaking here) *"I will not travel among you, for you are a stubborn and rebellious people. If I did, I would surely destroy you along the way."* (Exodus 33:3 NIV) Those that teach that God Himself travelled with the Israelites the whole time they were in the wilderness are only partially correct. There was actually a period of time when God separated Himself from the Israelites and did not travel among them for their own safety. That is how angry God became with them. Had it not been for His especially close friendship with Moses, there most certainly would have been no hope for the people of Israel after the golden calf incident.

The Levites, turning on their own brothers and sisters, should remind us that when we repent and commit our lives to serving Jesus, there will be things in our lives that must be cut out and cut off. Sometimes this is even a relationship in our own family. Again, I am not saying that you need to go home and slay your family if they aren't serving The Lord. No. Please don't do that. But, this Old Testament visual is a picture of what must occur in our hearts if we are to come before the Lord untainted.

So, this is the challenge I would like to present to you as

we close: Have you gone through your life already and made sure it is spotless? Have you gone through your relationships and made sure they are spotless? Have you gone through your finances and made sure they are spotless?

It is no surprise that once the Levites decided to follow after God that He had them remove every unclean tie from their midst. Worshippers, when we decide to follow Jesus we must do exactly the same.

FOOD FOR THOUGHT

QUESTION & ANSWER TIME

1. What in your life might not be pleasing to God?

2. Are there any relationships that keep you from pursuing God completely?

3. Who in your life is a Godly leader that can give you sound counsel and wisdom regarding things holding you back in your surrender to Jesus?

30

ه入

Holding up the Standard of the Levites - Part 2

C ontinuing from the previous chapter it is important I make you aware of the three key actions that qualified the Levites to become the special people who were allowed in God's presence. I believe these exact three things the Levites did long ago are what worship teams all around the world need to hear so desperately today.

Worshippers, being holy and pure before the Lord is not something we do so we can put stars on our behavior chart. It is something we do to make a place suitable for His presence. Sin is evidence that love for the presence of God has left, while righteousness, on the other hand, is evidence that love for His presence has come in. Let's look at the three qualifying actions of the Levites and see how they can apply to us today:

QUALIFYING ACTION I

Levites honor and associate with authority correctly, even in the desert place. Let's be real. It is hard to be honorable in the desert place of your life. The desert seasons of life can lead to desperation, and desperation can cause us to take desperate measures that really are not so wise. When in the place of desperation, it is even harder to act honorably toward someone in a position of authority when they ask you to do something difficult. This is exactly where a true Levite thrives. *"So he (Moses) stood at the entrance to the camp and said, 'Whoever is for the Lord, come to me.' And all the Levites rallied to him."* (Exodus 32:26 NIV)

First off, you must note that the Israelites were in the desert place when all of these things took place. It was the desert the Lord used to separate those who were for Him and those who were against Him. Likewise, it will always be the desert places of your life that God will use to reveal where your heart stands with Him and where it stands against Him. Isn't it interesting how God pulled Moses, the shepherd to the Israelite people, away from the Israelites to test them? If you ever feel like you are in a desert season, and God is being silent, just remember that a teacher does not talk when his students are being tested.

Secondly, you must note the power of association. Who

you associate yourself with will determine your eternal destination. The Levites had enough sense to know that Moses was God's appointed leader and that Moses was bound to God as a close friend. Therefore, if the Levites were to side with Moses, they would be in turn siding with God. Your associations are much more important and powerful than you think. Who do you most closely associate yourself with, and who has the most influence in your life? By your association with these people, you can determine exactly where your life is headed. There is safety in submission to healthy spiritual authority. Yet this generation does not believe in submission to authority, especially godly authority.

QUALIFYING ACTION II

Levites are people who repent quickly. They prefer pleasing the Lord to popularity. *"So he (Moses) stood at the entrance to the camp and said, 'Whoever is for the Lord, come to me.' And all the Levites rallied to him."* (Exodus 32:26 NIV) I cannot stress the weight of the above verse enough. You must first note that it does not say: "The Levites were the only ones found not worshipping the golden calf." No, it never says that, which suggests the Levites were more than likely worshipping the golden calf along with the rest of God's people. The Good News is that all have sinned and fallen short of the glorious standard of the

Lord (Romans 3:23) but unfortunately, out of all the tribes of Israel, the Levites were the only ones to repent and run back to the Lord.

Moses shouted: "Whoever is for the Lord, come to me." This was one of the first recorded public calls to repentance, much like a modern-day "altar call." The Lord is always looking for those who will willingly leave sin and repent, because He is gracious, merciful and forgiving. He is looking for people to use, people who will do great and mighty things for His Kingdom. And the good news is that these people do not have to come to Him already perfect. He has special places of service and authority reserved for all whose hearts are willing to be truly devoted to Him. What an honor this is.

Even in the light of God's mercy and forgiveness, not everyone in the desert place wanted to respond to the call of repentance made by Moses, and this would lead to the death of many of them. How do you respond when you know you have sinned against the Lord? Is your heart soft enough to run back to Jesus even if it separates you from the crowd and might not look cool? The Levites had soft hearts towards the Lord, and they were not worried about looking cool in front of their own brothers and sisters.

QUALIFYING ACTION III

Levites let God deal with their sin, even when it hurts. *"Then he said to them (the Levites), "This is what the Lord, the God of Israel, says: 'Each man strap a sword to his side. Go back and forth through the camp from one end to the other, each killing his brother and friend and neighbor.'" The Levites did as Moses commanded, and that day about three thousand of the people died. Then Moses said, "You have been set apart to the Lord today, for you were against your own sons and brothers, and he has blessed you this day."* (Exodus 32:27 NIV)

Even though it was painful, the Levites did not withhold anything from the Lord. Whatever was in their life that was refusing to yield to Jesus they did away with. A true Levite understands that sin must be killed and annihilated, not just from within, but also from around us. When a Levite repents, he goes through his entire house and does away with anything that may not be pleasing to the Lord. He does the same with his relationships, because a true Levite values pleasing God's heart over satisfying man's opinion.

The Levites understood the spiritual danger of being closely bound to those that did not want to follow Jesus. Each person who sided with the golden calf that day, and refused to repent, was like a walking time bomb, a spiritual terrorist, a danger to the safety of the whole camp. Sin is not a game. The Levites knew that these people had to go because there was no way they were going to be able to complete the journey to the Promised Land with them. So what is in your life that needs to be checked on or brushed up? How do you respond to the call of God to live a life of holiness? A calloused heart is unable to repent, while a soft heart responds to every last whisper of the Holy Spirit.

FOOD FOR THOUGHT
QUESTION & ANSWER TIME

1. How do you view spiritual authority?

2. When's the last time you examined your life and made sure everything was spotless before the Holy Spirit?

3. What in your life might God ask you to get rid of that may be difficult?

31

Closing - The Cry of My Heart

Give yourself a pat on the back, because we have just arrived at the end of the book. I hope it has been a blessing to you. I know many things in this book may have been challenging to take in, but as I said in the beginning, it is all for your benefit and blessing.

I hope that you have found a new understanding that will stretch your heart for God. I also hope that you have discovered some practical tools that will help you have a healthier and more effective worship team. As I said earlier in this book, there is nothing more that a church needs to inspire them to worship than to just see the face of Jesus.

As I close this book I would like to end with something I wrote about Jesus. Let your heart and mind imagine the picture I am presenting to you, and may you always be blessed with an ever deepening fellowship with the Father, Son and the Holy Spirit.

"The very heart of Heaven, the light that illuminates and warms the Holy City is the precious Son of God - Jesus. He is the core of everything that happens upon Mount Zion. In the city of our great King, He is the epicenter of beauty. Found in the eternal dwelling of the saints and angels is the Son of God – Jesus. He was the treasure hidden from before the foundation of the universe. He was there when the foundation of the Earth was laid, when the stars were spoken into existence. He is "I am." The Father smiles as He sits upon the throne watching His Son walk among His people. He forever will be Emmanuel, God with us.

We can touch Him, we can feel Him, and yes, we can embrace Him. Yes, with our own arms we can hold Him - we can hold God. We can look at Him in the eyes and see His eyes looking back into ours. What do we see when we look into His eyes? We see the fire of His love for us. We see His great compassion for His people, who are the sheep of His pasture.

When we stand before Him we will realize that not only can we look at Him and hold Him, but we can talk to Him face-to-face. We can stand right in front of Him and finally tell Him in person how much we love Him. We can tell Him in person how long we have waited for this moment. We can look at Him eye to eye and tear for tear sing our song to Him. He will wipe all our tears away. As eternity upon eternity passes by, His face will not grow dim. His face will shine forever – like a sun that never sets, His face will shine forever.

Jesus is worthy of all the praise, all the honor and all the glory forever and ever. He is the very reason the entire universe exists and He is the reason anything living has life. What a great God we serve and what a great God we worship. Give Him all that you are, and hold nothing back from Him. We love you forever Jesus! Amen!"

God bless you all, -Phil King

Keep In Touch!

I'd love to hear your comments, questions and feedback about the book and how it relates to what you're doing. Join me on Facebook at https://www.facebook.com/philkingmusic/

You can also learn more about my music and download chord charts for most of my worship music at my website: http://www.philkingmusic.com/

15089785R00101

Printed in Great Britain
by Amazon.co.uk, Ltd.,
Marston Gate.